An Epic Love Story

Patricia C. Vines

Copyright @2016

Patricia C. Vines

All rights reserved. No part of this book may be reproduced or transmitted in any form or by any means, electronic or mechanical, including photocopying, recording, or by any information storage and retrieval system, without permission in writing from the copyright owner or author.

The information in this book is for educational purposes only.

ISBN-13: 978-1532772351
ISBN-10: 1532772351

First Edition
Printed in the United States of America

Table of Contents

Dedication iv
Introduction v
Other Writings From This Author vi
Acknowledgments... vii
Chapter 1, Remember Love 1
Chapter 2, Banner was the Love 17
Chapter 3, Sought, But Found Him Not 27
Chapter 4, No Spot in Thee 35
Chapter 5, Permitted Communion 46
Chapter 6, Searching 63
Chapter 7, Heart Sealed 69
Chapter 8, Responsibility for Family 79
The 16 "Nevers of Communication with your Beloved" 88
Biography 90
7 Feast Of The LORD Being Symbolic Of New Life 91

Dedication

To John Ryan and
Our Daughter

Precious friend

My Sons – Michael, Christopher

My Daughter, Missy - "Christie"

My Granddaughter - Crystal

My Greatgrandchildren –

"Geremiah"

"Elena - Nickname, Twinkle"

Introduction

Love, sex, marriage and romance can serve as the ultimate Jekyll and Hyde of life. On one hand they give us great joy and satisfy, the deepest desires and needs, but such desires can also turn on us and plunge our lives into the deepest of pain. God has given us these desires, drives and needs and the guidance through "Song of Songs" to bless, enlighten and all of its delights and joys.

"The Art of Attraction"

Attraction is about being the person that God desires you to be and allowing God to bring to you the kind of person He knows is best for you, the one and only "soul mate."

Be it early or late in life, it is something that naturally happens when we run God's race together.

John 16:13;
13 But when he, the Spirit of truth, comes, he will guide you into all the truth. He will not speak on his own; he will speak only what he hears, and he will tell you what is yet to come. (NIV®)

Yeshua (Jesus) is The Rose of Sharon.

Song of Solomon 2:1;
1 I *am* the rose of Sharon, *and* the lily of the valley.

Other Writings From This Author

Here are some of the other works the author has published. That includes this book as well.

Eve And The Proverbs 31 Woman Series

Eve and the Proverbs 31 Woman
Are They? (Volume 2)

They Do Not Understand Series

I Luvs Ya
The Jewish Wedding (Volume 2)
The Cross, The Staff, The Crown (Volume 3)
I Will Lift Up Mine Eyes (Volume 4)
Garden of the Heart (Volume 5)
C-ing Bible History (Volume 6)
Everyday Life In Biblical Times (Volume 7)

Other Titles

An Epic Love Story

Acknowledgments

GOD'S WORD ® Translation is a registered trademark of GOD'S WORD® to the Nations, PO Box 400, Orange Park, Florida 32067-0400.

"Scripture quotations taken from the New American Standard Bible®, Copyright© 1960, 1962, 1963, 1968, 1971, 1972, 1973, 1975, 1977, 1995 by The Lockman Foundation Used by permission." (www.Lockman.org)

Scripture quotations are taken from the HOLY BIBLE, New Living Translation, copyright© 1996, 2004, 2007, 2013 by Tyndale House Foundation. Used by permission of Tyndale House Publishers, Inc., Carol Stream, Illinois 60188. All rights reserved.

Some of the Scripture quotations, in this publication are from the HOLY BIBLE, NEW INTERNATIONAL VERSION® NIV® Copyright© 1973, 1978, 1984, 2011 by Biblica, Inc.®. Used by permission. All rights reserved worldwide. The "NIV" and "New International Version" are trademarks registered in the United States Patent and Trademark Office by Biblica, Inc.®. Use of either trademark requires the permission of Biblica, Inc.®.

"Scripture quotations are from The Holy Bible, English Standard Version® (ESV®), copyright© 2001 by Crossway, a publishing ministry of Good News Publishers. Used by permission. All rights reserved."

Scripture quotations marked HCSB are taken from the Holman Christian Standard Bible®, Copyright© 1999, 2000, 2002, 2003 by Holman Bible Publishers. Used by permission. Holman Christian Standard Bible®, Holman CSB®, and HCSB® are federally registered trademarks of Holman Bible Publishers.

Scripture taken from the New King James Version®. Copyright© 1982 by Thomas Nelson, Inc. Used by permission. All rights reserved.

NET Bible copyright © 1996-2006 by Biblical Studies Press, L.L.C. http://netbible.com.

All pictures and information contained therein in this book is factual to the best of the author information and is presented for informational and entertainment purposes only.

Chapter One
Remember Love

It began in the late 50's. I was about 15 years of age and there he was, standing in front of me and said, "Hi, beautiful, may I carry your books!" It began as the "Art of Dating", then the "Art of Courtship", and then the "Art of Intimacy", on to the "Art of Romance", to the "Art of Conflict", to the "Art of Commitment" and approximately fifty-seven years of searching, always loving, always caring and always praying. Looking at each and every face in a crowd, always searching, always longing and then suddenly you see a picture that you know in your heart is the "soul mate", its him. Those gorgeous brown eyes, black hair that has faded to gray, face structure like precious chiseled marble – unable to keep your eyes off of him. "Song of Solomon 3:5b" ... that you will not arouse or awaken love, until it pleases."

Courtship is the beginning of sacrifice and commitment between two people. Dating could be described as "kicking tires" to be sure there is air, or "browsing in a store." Courtship is when the two people know the other is so **SPECIAL** and wanting to know more about them. Courtship is a risk between two people. And then intimacy that does not end as one expected creating conflict. Twenty-five percent of a relationship deals with intimacy (sex), twenty-five percent deals with conflict or it may end with a rainbow of color. The other fifty percent? When the man kisses the woman and she kisses him – they are betrothed, the marriage has begun. It brings different thoughts, views, opinions and other aspects of bringing two blocks of granite together. Marriage, with all of its joys and struggles can become the most beautiful statue of two people ever created. "My beloved is dazzling and ruddy, outstanding among ten thousand." His lips are like lilies, his hands are of steel and velvet. His abdomen is carved ivory inlaid with sapphires and his legs are pillars of alabaster set in pure gold." Then we come to the "Art of

Romance". Many relationships fail because two people become forgetful and lazy. The "Art of Romance" is that of a gardener. When someone decided to plant a garden, there is the thrill of seeing how beautiful it will become. The appreciation and enjoyment of it lasts for a season. But, inevitably, weeds and other destructive forces begin to take their toll on the flowers and foods. Does the gardener sit back, watch this happen and wish for it to die? No. They must work to improve and protect the relationship.

The couple do not get bored with one another. His appreciation of her is a constant process, just as her respect for him grows greater every day. Commitment is having perseverance and perspective to make it last a lifetime. Her desire to be a "Comfort, Counterpart and Completer" for him is first and foremost in her life. But, for example, when a person is learning to sky dive he or she must be committed to jump out of the plane long before ever getting into it. If a person is not committed to jump, think of the very tempting option to scream, "FORGET IT!" The fear of the jump would paralyze him or her and he would never experience the joy and rush of "flying." Marriage and commitment is much the same. The commitment for a lifetime will give abundant joy far beyond our expectations

The "Art of Commitment" is the most important aspect of the sovereignty of God in our lives. God is the all-knowing, the all-loving, and the all-powerful One. He is the creator of all and He knows what is best for everyone. It is God who brings this initial attraction to the JOY of sex to a lifelong commitment. In order for all of life to work properly – Yeshua (Jesus) must be your Lord and Savior. God's best can be ultimately, deeply fulfilled. The couple, they can become God's blessing to each other.

It brings us to the "Song of Songs" - "We will be glad and rejoice in thee, we will remember thy love more than wine." Chapter 1:4.

The Song of Songs is a little book which has had a

peculiar attraction for many of the people of God all through the centuries, and others of them have had great difficulty in understanding just why such a book should have a place in the canon of Holy Scripture at all. Frequently I have heard those who, it seemed to me, ought to have known better, say that as far as they were concerned they could see nothing of spiritual value in this little book, and that they questioned very much whether it were really entitled to be considered as part of the inspired Word of God. As far as that is concerned, it is not left to the Congregation in our day to decide which books should belong to the canon of Scripture and which should be omitted. Our blessed Yeshua (Jesus) has SETTLED that for us, at least as far as the Old Testament is concerned. When He was here on earth He had exactly the same Old Testament that we have, consisting of the same books, no more and no less.

Those that are sometimes called the Apocryphal books did not belong to the Hebrew Old Testament which He valued and fed upon, and which He commended to His disciples, and, more than that, upon which He placed His divine imprimatur when He referred to the entire volume and said, "The Scripture cannot be broken." Therefore we do not have to raise any question as to the inspiration of the Canticles. He declared the Hebrew bible to be the Word of the living God, and there are many figures from this little book in various parts of the New Testament; for instance, *"the well of living water"* (John 4); *"the veiled woman"* (1 Cor. 11); *"the precious fruit"* (James 5:7); *"the spotless bride"* (Ephesians 5:27); *"unquenchable love"* (1 Cor. 13:8); *"love strong as death"* (John 15:13); *"ointment poured forth"* (John 12:3); *"draw me"* (John 6:44); *"the Shepherd leading His flock"* (John 10:4,5,27); *and "the fruits of righteousness"* (Phil. 1:11). Who can fail to see in all these allusions to the "Song of Songs?"

If we grant that it is inspired, what then are its lessons? Why do we have it in Holy Scripture? Many of the Jewish teachers thought of it simply as designed of God to give a right apprehension of conjugal love. They thought of it as the glorification of the bliss of wedded life, and if we conceived of it from no higher standpoint than this, it would mean that it had a right to a place in the canon. Wedded life in Israel represented the very highest and fullest and deepest affection at a time when, in the nations surrounding Israel, women were looked upon a <u>mere chattel, as a slave, or as the object of man's pleasure to be discarded when and as he pleased.</u> But it was otherwise in Israel. The JEWISH HOME WAS A PLACE WHERE LOVE AND TENDERNESS REIGNED, and no doubt this little book had a great deal to do with lifting it to that glorious height.

But down through the centuries, the more spiritually minded in Israel saw a deeper meaning in this "Song of Songs"; they recognized the design of God to set forth the mutual love subsisting between Yeshua and Israel. Again and again, in other scriptures, Yeshua (Jesus) is likened to a *bridegroom,* Israel to His chosen bride, and so the spiritual in Israel, in the years before Yeshua, came to look at the song in this way. They called it *"The Book of Communion."* It is the book that sets forth Yeshua and His people in blessed and happy communion. And then all through the Christian centuries those who have had an insight into spiritual truth have thought of it from two standpoints. <u>First</u> as typifying the wondrous relationship that subsists between Yeshua and the church, the glowing heart, the enraptured spirit of our blessed Lord revealing Himself to His redeemed people as her Bridegroom and her Head, and the Church's glad response. And then, <u>second</u>, looking at it from a moral standpoint, as setting forth the relationship between an individual soul and Yeshua, how many a devoted saint has exclaimed with gladness, **"Oh, I am my Beloved's and His desire is toward me."**

Rutherford's meditations were evidently based on this little book when he exclaimed:

> "Oh, I am my Beloved's,
> And my Beloved's mine.
> He brings a poor vile sinner
> Into His house of wine;
> I stand upon His merit,
> I know no safer stand,
> Not even where glory dwelleth
> In Immanuel's land."

Therefore we may think of the book from four standpoints.

One: Looking at it literally, we see the glorification of wedded love.

Two: Looking at it from a dispensational standpoint, we see the relationship between Yeshua and Israel.

Three: Redemptive, we find the wonderful relationship between Yeshua and the Church.

Four: And studying it from the moral or spiritual standpoint we see it as the book of communion between an individual soul and the blessed, glorified, risen Lord.

It is a bit difficult to get the exact connection of the different portions of the book. It is not a drama, as the book of Job is. It does not present to our consideration any continued story. It consists rather of a series of love lyrics, each one complete in itself. It is the lover with heart enraptured setting to music the thrill of the soul, and thus you have the cluster of **song-flowers**, each one setting forth some different phrase of communion between the beloved and the one so loved. And yet, back of it all, there must be some kind of story. What is this background?

Something like a hundred years ago, Ewald, the great German critic, who has been called the father of higher criticism, suggested that the story was something like this. In the hill country North of Jerusalem there was a family in charge of a vineyard belonging to King Solomon. The young shepherdess had been won by a shepherd who had drawn her heart to himself, and their troth had been plighted for they had kissed. But King Solomon, as he rode along the lane one day, saw this young shepherdess in the vineyard, and his heart went out to her. He determined to win her for himself, and so tried by blandishment to stir up her affections. But she was true to her sylvan admirer. By-and-by the King actually had her kidnapped and taken to his palace, to the royal harem, and there again and again he pressed his suit and tried to alienate her from her shepherd lover in the hills. Sometimes she was almost tempted to yield, for her case seemed a hopeless one, but then she would remember him, her former lover, and she would say, "No, I cannot turn from him. 'I am my beloved's, and his desire is toward me.'" Eventually, King Solomon set her free and she went back to the one she loved.

This view of kidnapping first and foremost, would make King Solomon "the villain of the piece," and when we turn to the Word of God, we find that Solomon is viewed by the Holy Spirit of God as a type of the Lord Jesus Christ, (Yeshua). In the Psalms Solomon is portrayed as the prince of peace succeeding David after years of warfare, and setting forth Yeshua coming again to reign as Prince of Peace. In the Renewed Testament the Lord Jesus (Yeshua) says, **"The queen of the south shall rise up in the judgment with this generation, and shall condemn it; for she came from the uttermost parts of the earth to hear the wisdom of Solomon; and behold, a greater than Solomon is here"** - Matthew 12:42. When Solomon is described as a type of Yeshua it is not personal. Whenever any man is spoken of as a type of Yeshua, we are not to think of what the man is in himself, but what he is officially. David officially was a type of Yeshua. David personally was guilty of very grievous sin, but the Lord is the sinless One. Solomon was guilty of very serious departure from God during certain periods of his life, but officially he represented our Yeshua as the 'Prince of Peace.' It was not the way of the Spirit of God to present a character, or some other animate or inanimate object, as a type of Yeshua in one place and a type of that which is wicked and unholy in another; and if we were to take Ewald's suggestion as the real story behind the book, we would have to think of Solomon as the type of the world, the flesh, satan and trying to win the heart of his young woman away from the shepherd who represents our Messiah, Yeshua.

We need to understand some of the most lovely and tender passages of this little book in which the King addresses himself to the shepherdess, as mere blandishment instead of a sincere and holy love. These very passages are those which down through the centuries have thrilled the heart of the people of God. They have reveled in them, they have delighted in them, and fed their souls upon them. It is not likely that they have been misled, that the Holy spirit who came to guide into all truth has thus deceived, or allowed to be deceived, so many of God's most spiritual people throughout the centuries, and therefore, it is refused to take the story which came from Ewald as the explanation of the "Song of Songs."

Here is another story that I was privileged to experience. I was alone on my knees and needing to teach this precious book, I found it a bit perplexing. Not liking the story or explanation of Edwald, I went to the ONE whom wrote the book and asked Him to tell me what was behind it. "OH," you say, "DID YOU KNOW THE AUTHOR OF THE BOOK?" Yes, I have known HIM since 1973 of the 10th day of March when we meet in a little "Dutch Country Baptist Church." "WELL," you say, "THE BOOK IS RATHER A RECENT THING IF YOU KNOW THE AUTHOR." No, not at all, it is a very OLD BOOK; but the author is the ANCIENT OF DAYS and I have known Him ever since in grace HE converted my soul. This meeting with Yeshua took place many, many years after meeting the "soul mate" of my days, my first and only human deep abiding, unending love. And so I take Yeshua at His word and remind Him occasionally of His promise that when the Holy Spirit came, He would take of the things of Yeshua and show them unto us; and I said, **"Blessed Yeshua, I am somewhat perplexed about this wonderful little book; by the Spirit will you show to me the real understanding of its meaning. Thank you!"** I will strive to give it to you as He gave it to me. You may not think I am correct and that is your privilege. If that is your belief, then please ask Him about it, and if He tells you something different, it would be a privilege to correct it if I am wrong.

This is what I thought I saw behind it all. Up there in the North country, in the mountain district of Ephraim, King Solomon had a vineyard (we are told that in the 11th verse of the last chapter), and he let it out to keepers, to an Ephraimite family. Apparently the husband and father was dead, but there was a Mother and at least two brothers, two sons. We read, "My mother's children (sons), but there were at least two. And then there were two daughters, two sisters, a little one spoken of in the 8th chapter - "We have a little sister." she was a little undeveloped one. And then here was the older daughter, the Shulamite. It would seem as though this one was to be considered the "ugly duckling," or the "Cinderella" of the family. Regardless of attitude, her brothers did not appreciate her and forced hard tasks upon her, denying her the privilege that a growing girl might have expected in a Hebrew home. "My mother's sons were angry with me." That makes me wonder if they were not her half-brothers, if this were not a divided family.

"My mother's sons were angry with me; they made me the keeper of the vineyards; but mine own vineyard have I not kept." (This was my experience for approximately 57 years). Her brothers said to her, "No, you cannot loll around this house; you get out and get to work. Look after the vineyard." She was responsible to prune the vines and to set

An Epic Love Story

the traps for the little foxes that spoiled the vines. They also committed to her care of the lambs and the kids of the flock. It was her responsibility to protect and find suitable pasture for them. She worked hard, and was in the sun from early till late. "Mine own vineyard have I not kept." She meant, "While working so hard in the field, I have no opportunity to look after myself." What girl is here that does not value a few hours in front of the looking-glass, the opportunity to fix her hair and to beautify herself in any lawful way? She had no opportunity to care for her own person and so she says, "My own vineyard have I not kept." Circumstances had created a mind set of "I am not worthy." I really do not suppose that she knew the need for cosmetics of any kind; or clothes, or shoes and yet from time to time she would remember the 'Shepherd' and his love. Every now and then she would see beautiful ladies as she caught a glimpse of them, or as she bent over a spring and saw her own reflection, she would say, "I am sunburned but comely, and if I only had the opportunity to find him again I could be as beautiful as he said I was, like the rest of the ladies. This is all involved in that expression, "Mine own vineyard have I not kept."

She dreamed that one day as she was caring for her flock she would look up, and to her amazement there would stand the handsome 'Shepherd' whom believed that she was "beautiful." He would gaze intently upon her and she would exclaim, "Look not upon me, because I am black, because the sun hath looked upon me." And then she gives the explanation, "My mother's children (sons) were angry with me; they made me the keeper of the vineyards; but mine own vineyard have I not kept." She felt no need. But she dreams of him saying quietly without any offensive forwardness, "I was not thinking of you as swarthy and sunburnt and unpleasant to look upon. To my mind you are altogether lovely' behold, thou art fair, my love; there is no spot in thee." Of course that went a long way back toward a friendship or the "Art of Dating" and so little by little that

"Art" ripened into "Courtship", then "Intimacy", then "Romance" and then affection into a glorious love and finally, the 'Shepherd' had won the heart of this very lonely shepherdess. Then she sent him away, but before he went, he declared, "Someday I am coming for you, and I am going to make you my own, my bride." And she dreamed and she forgot and then by and by she remembered, she believed. Probably no one else did, her brothers did not believe her, her family did not believe her, the people in the mountain country felt that she was a poor simple country maiden who had been deceived by this strange marvelous man for he was long gone. She had inquired of him where he fed his flock, but they put her off with an evasive answer, "No one knows of him." But she continued to dream and would exclaim, **"the voice of my beloved,"** no other has his aroma. Then back to reality where all was quiet and dark about her. But she still trusted in her heart of hearts as her love and caring for him deepened. She was silent.

Then one day there was a great cloud of dust on the road and the country people ran to see what it meant. Here came a glorious cavalcade. There was the King's body-guard and the King himself, and they stopped just opposite the vineyard. To the amazement of the shepherdess, the royal outriders came to her with the announcement, **"The king has sent us for you."** "For me?" she asked. **"Yes, come."** And in obedience she went, (for she had always been obedient), and when she looked into the face of the King, behold, the King was the 'Shepherd' who had won her heart and she said, **"I am my beloved's and his desire is toward me."**

The greatest reason I think this is the story of the Canticles is because all the way through this wondrous volume, from Genesis to Revelation, we have the story of the 'Shepherd' who came from the far country, from heaven's highest glory down into this dark world that He might woo and win the bride for Himself. And then He went away, but He said, **"I will come again, and receive you unto Myself."**

And so His congregation has waited long for Him to come back, but some day He is coming to fulfill His word, and:

"When He comes, the glorious King,
All His ransomed home to bring.
Then anew this song we'll sing,
'Hallelujah, what a Savior!'"

And so I think that is the background of the expression of loving communion in this little book, the "Song of Songs". You notice that very title reminds you of the Holy of Holies; it is the transcendent song. The Jews did not allow a young man to read this little book until he was thirty years of age, lest he might read into it mere human voluptuousness and misuse its beautiful phrases, and so we say it is only as we grown in grace and in the knowledge of Yeshua that we can read this book understandingly and see in it the secret of the LORD.

I think the first chapter divides itself into THREE parts. The first four verses give us the soul's satisfaction. It is the expression of the bride's delight in her bridegroom. She exclaims, "The Song of Songs," which is Solomon's. Let Him kiss me with the kisses of His mouth: for Thy love is better than wine." There was a dear servant of God once said, "I have sometimes wished there were only one masculine personal pronoun in the world, so that every time I say, **'Him,'** everyone would know I mean Yeshua. You remember Mary Magdalene saying, "They have taken away my Lord, and I know not where they have laid Him." Then, looking up to the one she supposed to be the gardener, she said, "Sir, if thou have borne Him hence, tell me where thou hast laid Him, and I will take Him away." She did not think it necessary to use the name Yeshua. There was only ONE to her and that was the Lord who had redeemed her; and so the enraptured soul says, **"Oh, my soul, to enjoy His love, His communion; to enjoy the blessedness of finding** satisfaction in Himself." "Because of the savor of Thy good ointments Thy name is as ointment poured forth, therefore do the virgins love Thee." We are reminded how the house was filled with the odor of the ointment when Mary broke her alabaster box and poured it upon His head.

> "How sweet the name of Yeshua sounds
> In a believer's ear!
> It soothes his sorrows, heals his wounds,
> And drives away his fear."

And now the heart cries out, "Draw me, we will run after thee: the King hath brought me into His chambers: we will be glad and rejoice in thee, we will remember thy love more than wine: the upright love Thee." The shepherdess has been brought from the hill country into the royal palace, as you and I from the distant country into the very presence of the Lord Himself, and how often our hearts have sung:

> "I am Thine, O Lord, I have heard Thy voice,
> And it told thy love to me;
> But I long to rise in the arms of faith,
> And be closer drawn to Thee."

> "Draw me nearer, nearer, nearer, blessed Lord,
> To the tree (cross) where Thou hast died;
> Draw me nearer, nearer, nearer, blessed Lord,
> To thy precious bleeding side."

"We will run after thee: the King hath brought me into his chambers: we will be glad and rejoice in Thee, we will remember Thy love more than wine." She has been claimed by the King, her soul mate. What a wonderful picture we have here of real communion. No one has ever entered into the truth of communion with Yeshua until He Himself has become the all-absorbing passion of the soul. His love transcends every earthly joy, of which wine is the symbol in Scripture. Why is it so used? Because of its exhilarating character. Wine speaks of anything of earth which stimulates or cheers. When a world-ling is cast down and depressed, he says, "Give strong drink unto him that is ready to perish, and wine unto those that be of heavy hearts. Let him drink and forget his poverty, and remember his misery no more – Proverbs 31:6,7. And so wine speaks of the joys of earth to which we once turned before we knew Yeshua. But after we know Him, we say, "We will remember Thy love more than wine." For that reason I am always grieved in spirit when some Christian comes with the old, old question, "Do you think there is any harm in this or that? Any harm in the theater, in dancing, in a game of cards, in a social party that has no place for Yeshua?" I say, "If you only really knew Him, and kept the law (Torah) and kept the commandments and loved Him with all your heart, soul and strength then the question would never be asked again. "We will remember Thy love more than wine." One minute spent in fellowship with Him is worth all the joys and pleasures of earth. That is what this little book of love is designed to teach us.

There is a fullness in His love, a sweetness found in fellowship with Yeshua, of which the world-ling knows nothing. If you are in Yeshua, these things fall off like withered autumn leaves. I often hear people singing:

> "Oh, how I love Jesus,
> Oh, how I love Jesus,
> Oh, how I love Jesus,
> Because He first loved me!"

And yet the same people who sing those things sometimes never spend half-an-hour a day over the Bible; never spend ten minutes alone with God in prayer; have very little interest in the coming together of the Lord's people to wait on Him. Invite them to a prayer-meeting and they are never there, but invite them to a social evening and they are all present. It is evident that the love of Yeshua is not yet the controlling passion of the heart. The surrendered soul exclaims, "We will remember Thy love more than wine." And in Ephesians we read, "Be not drunk with wine, wherein is excess, but be filled with the Spirit." The Spirit-filled believer never craves the follies of the godless world. **Yeshua is enough to satisfy at all times.**

Song of Songs: Chapter 1: 1-4
1. The song of songs, which is Solomon's.
   (A Young Bride, a Shulamite girl)
   (The Shulamite speaks)
2. Let him kiss me with the kisses of his mouth. For thy love better than wine.
   (The Daughters of Jerusalem speak)
3. Because of the savor of thy good ointments thy name is *like* ointments poured forth; therefore do the virgins love thee.
   (The Shulamite speaks)
4. Draw me after thee. We will make haste, the king hath brought me into his chambers. We will be glad and rejoice in thee; we will remember thy love more than wine. The upright love thee.

We cannot get to know our soul mate or Him unless we invest time together, to learn who we are or they are. It is a process of time, cultivation and restraint.

It brings us to the next section (SECOND) which takes in verses five to eleven. This looks back to the time when she first met her lover and inquired of him as to where he fed his flock. He answered, **"If thou know not, O thou fairest among women, go thy way forth by the footsteps of the flock, and feed thy kids beside the shepherds' tent."** In other words, it is as when the disciples of John came to Yeshua and said, "Master, where dwellest Thou?" And He said, **"Come and see."** And so the soul cried out, **"O thou shepherd of my heart feedest Thou?"** And he said to her, **"Just go along in the shepherds' path, feed your flock with the rest, and you will find out."** If you take the path of devotedness to Yeshua, you will soon know where He dwells. If you walk in obedience to His Word you cannot fail to find Him.

Chapter 1:5-11
(The Shulamite speaks)
5. I am black, but comely, O ye daughters of Jerusalem, like the tents of Kedar, like the curtains of Solomon.
6. Look not upon me, because I am black, because the sun hath looked upon me. My mother's children were angry with me; they made me the keeper of the vineyards, but mine own vineyard have I not kept.

(The Perplexed Bride, 1:7-8 – The Shulamite continues)
7. Tell me, O thou whom my soul loveth, where thou feedest, where thou makest thy flock to rest at noon; for why should I be like one that turneth aside by the flocks of thy companions,

(Solomon, the shepherd-lover, replies)
8. If thou know not, O thou fairest among women, go thy way in the footsteps of the flock, and feed thy kids beside the shepherds' tents.

(Solomon speaks)
9. I have compared thee, O my love, to a company of horses in Pharaoh's chariots.
10. Thy cheeks are comely with rows of *jewels*, thy neck with chains *of gold*.

(The daughters of Jerusalem speak)
11. We will make Thee borders of gold with studs of silver.

In the verses twelve to seventeen we have a wonderful

picture of communion with the king. There he and his beautiful bride are together in the royal palace, and she says, **"While the King sitteth at his table"** - and the table is the place of communion - **"my spikenard sendeth forth the smell thereof. A bundle of myrrh is my well-beloved unto me."** In other words, **"He is to me like a fragrant nosegay in which my senses delight."** And so we enter into communion with Yeshua. He becomes all in all to us and the heart goes out in worship and praise, like Mary, as already mentioned, in the house of Bethany bringing her alabaster box of ointment and pouring it on the head of Yeshua. The King sat at the table that day, and her spikenard sent forth its fragrance and the house was filled with the odor of the ointment. That is the worshiper. There can be no real worship excepting as the heart is occupied with Him.

It is common nowadays to substitute service for worship, and to be more taken up with hearing sermons or with ritual observances than with adoration and praise. God has said, **"Whoso offereth praise glorifieth Me."** He tells us He swells amide the praises of His people. It is the satisfied heart that really worships. When the soul has been won for Yeshua there will be appreciation of Himself for what He is; not merely thanksgiving (important as that is) for what He has so graciously bestowed upon us. **"Whom having not seen, ye love; in whom, though now ye see Him not, yet believing, ye rejoice with joy unspeakable and full of glory."** This causes the spirit to go out to Him in worship and praise.

"The Father," Jesus told the Samaritan woman, **"seeketh such to worship Him."** He yearns for the adoring love of devoted hearts. May we indeed respond to His desire and ever **"worship Him in spirit and in truth."**

(The Shulamite speaks)
    12. While the king *sitteth* at his table, my spikenard sendeth forth the fragrance thereof.
    13. A bundle of myrrh is my well-beloved unto me; he

shall lie all night between my breasts.
14. My beloved is unto me as a cluster of henna flowers in the vineyards of Engedi.
(Solomon responds)
15. Behold, thou *art* fair my love,; behold, thou art fair; thou *hast* doves' eyes.
(The Shulamite speaks)
16. Behold, thou *art* fair, my beloved, yea, pleasant; also out bed is green.
17. The beams of our house are cedar *and* our rafters of fir.

Chapter Two
Banner was the Love

"He brought me to the banqueting house, and his banner over me was love"
Song of Songs 2:4

The figure of the bride and the bridegroom is used very frequently in Scripture. Isaiah in the Old Testament says, **"As the bridegroom rejoiceth over the bride, so shall thy God rejoice over Thee."**

It is used by the Congregation in the Renewed Covenant (Testament). **"Christ loved the Church and gave Himself for it; that He might sanctify and cleanse it with the washing of water by the Word."** And when the apostle Paul speaks of the divine institution of marriage he says, **"For this cause shall a man leave his father and mother, and shall be joined unto his wife, and they two shall be one flesh. This is a great mystery: but I speak concerning Christ and the Church."** And then writing to the Corinthian believers, he says, **"I have espoused you to one husband, that I may present you as a chaste virgin to Christ."** Therefore, this delightful figure of the sweet and intimate marriage relationship is used throughout Scripture to set forth our union and communion with the Eternal Lover of our souls.

I have said that the Song of Songs is the Book of Communion. We have that beautifully set forth in the first seven verses of this second chapter. The Bride and the Bridegroom are conversing together. We delight to speak with those whom we love. One of the wonderful things about love is that when someone has really filled the vision of your soul, you do not feel than any time that is taken up communing with him or her is wasted. Here then you have the lovers out in the country together and she exclaims, for it is evidently she who speaks in verse one, **"I am the rose of Sharon, and the lily of the valleys."** Generally we apply those words to the blessed Lord; we speak of Him as the ROSE OF SHARON. We sing sometimes, **"He's the Lily of the Valley, the Bright and Morning Star."** It is perfectly right and proper to apply all of these delightful figures to Him, for we cannot find any figure that speaks of that which is beautiful and of good report that cannot properly be applied to the Lord. But the wonderful thing is that He has put His own beauty upon His people. And so here the bride is looking up into the face of the bridegroom saying, **"I am the rose (really, the narcissus, a blood-red flower) of Sharon, and the lily of the valleys"** - the lily that thrives in the hidden place, not in the town, not in the heat and bustle of the city, but out on the cool country-side, in the quiet field. Does it not speak of the soul's separation to Christ Himself?

It is when we draw apart from the things of the world, apart to Himself, that we really thrive and grow in grace and become beautiful in His sight. I am afraid that many of us do not develop spiritually as we should, because of the fact that we know so little of this heart-separation to Himself. One of the great grieves that comes to the heart of many a one who is seeking to lead others on in the ways of Yeshua, is to know the influence that the world has upon them after they are converted to God. How often the question comes from dear young Christians, "Must I give up this, and must I give up that, if I am going to live a consistent Christian life?" And the things that they speak of which such apparent yearning are mere trifles after all as compared with communion with Him. Must I give up eating sawdust in order to enjoy a good dinner? Who would talk like that? Must I give up the pleasures of the world in order that I may have communion with Yeshua? It is easy to let them all go if the soul is enraptured with Him; and when you get to know Him better, when you learn to enjoy communion with Him, you will find yourself turning the question around; and when the world says, "Won't you participate with us in this doubtful pleasure or in this unholy thing?" Your answer will be, "Must I give up so much to come down to that level? Must I give up communion with Him? Must I give up the enjoyment of His Word?

Must I give up fellowship with His people in order to go in the ways of the world?" That would be the giving up. Dear young Christian, do not think of it as giving up anything to go apart with Him and enjoy His blessed fellowship. It is then the separated soul looks into His face and says, **"I am like the narcissus of Sharon, and the lily of the valleys,"** and He at once responds, **"As the lily among thorns, so is My love among the daughters."** It is the heart-satisfaction that He has in His people.

See the contrast between the beautiful, fragile, lovely lily and the rough, unpleasant, disagreeable thorn. The thorn speaks of those who are still under the curse, walking in the ways of the world, and the lily sets forth His sanctified, devoted people, those who have turned from the world to Himself. This is His estimate of His saints, and as this little colloquy goes on, for it is just the soul speaking to Him and He responding, a beautiful, a beautiful holy dialogue, the bride looks up and says, **"As the apple-tree among the trees of the wood, so is My Beloved among the sons. I sat down under His shadow with great delight, and His fruit was** sweet to my taste." He says to her, "**You are like a lily to Me in contrast to the thorns.**" And she says, "**And You to me are like a beautiful fruit-tree in contrast to the fruitless trees of the wood.**" Many scholars have wondered just what word should be used here to translate the name of this tree. Is it the apple-tree that we know, or is it the citron, a tree of a beautiful, deep green shade, producing a lovely fruit, like a cross between our grapefruit and orange, a most refreshing fruit? But the thought that the bride expresses is this: You are so much more to me than any other can possibly be. I have shade and rest and refreshment in your presence. "**I sat down under His shadow with great delight, and His fruit was sweet to my taste.**"

How often the Spirit of God employs the figure of a shadow. To understand it aright you have to think of a hot eastern climate, the tropical sun shining down upon a wayfarer. Suddenly he sees before him a place of refuge, and exclaims as David does in the seventeenth Psalm, "**Keep me as the apple of the eye, hide me under the shadow of Thy wings.**" Again in Psalm 36:7, "**How excellent is Thy loving kindness, O God! Therefore the children of men put their trust under the shadow of Thy wings.**"

Isaiah speaks of "**the shadow of a great rock in a weary land.**" The figure is used very frequently in the Bible in speaking of rest and of comfort found alone in communion with Yeshua.

There is no drudgery here. You married folk, do you remember when you first fell in love with the one who afterward became your life-companion? Did you find it hard to spend half-an-hour with him? Did you try to find an excuse for staying away from the young man or lady? Did you always have some other engagement so that you would not be at home when the young man called on you? No; but you tried to put everything else out of the way so as to have the opportunity to become better acquainted with the person who had won your heart. So it is with the believer. The more we get to know of Yeshua the more we delight in His presence. So the Bride says, **"I sat down under His shadow with great delight, and His fruit was sweet to my taste."** Her bliss was complete.

"Delight thyself also in the Lord, and He shall give thee the desires of thine heart." You cannot delight in Yeshua if you are going after the things of the world. **"No man can serve two masters: for either he will hate the one, and love the other; or else he will hold to the one, and despise the other. Ye cannot serve God and mammon." Matthew 6:24.** So you cannot enjoy Yeshua and the world at the same time.

Then we go a step farther in this scene of communion. **"He brought me to the banqueting-house, and His banner over me was love."** This is the place of the soul's deep enjoyment when all else is shut out, and Yeshua all-satisfying love fills the spirit's vision, and the entire being is taken up with Himself. This is indeed the **"house of wine,"** the rest of love.

Song of Songs – Chapter 2:1-4
(The Shulamite is Comforted and she speaks)
1. I AM the rose of Sharon, and the lily of the valleys.(Solomon speaks)
2. As the lily among thorns, so is my love among the daughters.
(The Shulamite speaks)
3. As the apple tree among the trees of the wood, so is my beloved among the sons. I sat down under his shadow with great delight, and his fruit *was* sweet to my taste.
4. He brought me to the banquet house, and his banner over me *was* love.
5. Sustain me with cake of raisins, comfort me with apples; for I *am* sick with love.
6. His left hand is under my head, and his right hand

doth embrace me.

In verses five and six you have the soul so completely enthralled by the one who has won her heart that she does not care to think of anything else. It is the beginning of sacrifice and commitment. It's when two people know that the other is so valuable and special that no other could take their place. Then in verse seven we have his tender answer, for it is the Bridegroom speaking now: **vs. 7 - "I charge you, O ye daughters of Jerusalem, by the roes, and by the hinds of the field, that ye stir not up, nor awake my love, till she please, (not "till he please).**" The word is in the feminine, and the point is this, he sees such joy in His people when they are in communion with Him that He says, **"Now do not bring in anything to spoil this until she herself please."** That is illustrated in the Gospels. Yeshua had gone to the house of Mary, Martha, and Lazarus, and Martha served and was encumbered about her serving. But Mary took her place at the feet of Yeshua and listened to His every word. She was in the banqueting house and His banner over her was love. He was enjoying communion with her. But Martha said, "I have something more important for Mary than that; it is more important that she put the dishes on the table and get the dinner ready." But Yeshua said, as it were, **"Martha, Martha, I charge you that ye stir not up, nor awake my love till she please."** In other words, **"As long as she is content to sit at My feet and commune with Me, this means more to Me than the most enjoyable repast."**

When the poor Samaritan woman came to Him at the well outside the city of Sychar, his disciples came and wondered if He were not hungry, but He said, "I have meat to eat that ye know not of." It meant more to Him to have that poor sinner listening to His words, and drawing near to Him and entering into the love of His heart, than to enjoy the food that they had gone to the city to get. Service is a wonderful thing; it is a great thing to labor for so good a Master. But oh, there is something that comes before service, something that means more to Him and should mean more to us, and that is fellowship with Himself!

A husband and father was bereft of his precious wife and had just a darling daughter left to him. In those lonely days after the wife had passed away, he found his solace and his comfort in this beautiful girl she had left behind, and evening after evening when he came home from work, they would have their quiet little meal together, and then after the dishes had been put away they would go into the sitting-room, and talk or read, and enjoy each other's company. But now it was getting on toward the holiday season, and one evening after doing up the dishes, the daughter said, "Now, Father dear, you will excuse me tonight, I have something to occupy me upstairs. You can read while I go up." So he sat alone, and the next night the same thing happened, and night after night for about two weeks he sat alone each evening. On Yeshua birth morning the girl came bounding into his room saying, "Merry Yeshua Birthday, Father dear," and handed him a beautiful pair of slippers she had made for him. He looked at them, and then kissed her and said, "My darling, you made these yourself?" "Yes, Father." "Is this why I have been denied your company the last two weeks?" he asked. "Yes," she said; "this is my secret." Then he said, "That is very lovely, but next time I would rather have you than anything you can make for me." Our blessed Lord wants ourselves. Our heart's affection means far more to Him than service. And yet there will be service, of course, but service that springs out of communion, and that accomplishes a great deal more than when we are too busy to enjoy fellowship with Him.

Chapter 2: 8-13
(The Shulamite Describes a Happy Visit)
8. The voice of my beloved! Behold, he cometh leaping upon the mountains, skipping upon the hills.

An Epic Love Story

9. My beloved is like a roe or a young hart; behold, he standeth behind our wall, he looketh forth at the windows, gazing through the lattice.
(The Shulamite reports Solomon's words)
10. My beloved spoke, and said unto me, Rise up, my love, my fair one and come away.
11. For, lo, the winter is past, the rain is over *and* gone.
12. The flowers appear on the earth; come, and the voice of the turtledove is heard in our land.
13. The fig tree putteth forth her green figs, and the vines *with* the tender grapes give *forth* fragrance. Arise, my love, my fair one, and come away. (blameless and flawless)

These verses we may call "Love's Expectation." In this section he is absent from her and she is waiting for him to return. Suddenly she thinks she hears his voice, and she springs up saying, **"The voice of my beloved! Behold, he cometh leaping upon the mountains, skipping upon the hills."** You and I know His grace realize something of what this means. He has saved us, won our hearts, as this shepherd lover won the heart of this shepherdess, and He has gone away, but He said, **"I will come again, and receive you unto Myself,"** and when He comes, He will be the glorious King. It was the Shepherd who won her heart; it was the King to whom she was wedded. And so Yeshua, the Good Shepherd, has won us for Himself, but He will be the King when we sit with Him upon the throne.

Does it not stir your soul to think that at any moment we may hear His voice saying, **"Arise, My love, and come away?"** Listen to the way she depicts it here. **"My beloved spoke and said unto me, Rise up, my love, my fair one, and come away. For, lo, the winter is past, the rain is over and gone, the flowers appear on the earth; the time of the singing is come and the voice of the turtledove is heard in our land; the fig tree putteth forth her green figs, and the**

vines with the tender grape give a good smell. Arise, my love, my fair one, and come away." It is not merely the singing of birds, as you have it in other versions of scripture, but **"the time of singing,"** when He will sing and we shall sing, and we shall rejoice together, when earth's long winter of sorrow and trial and perplexity is ended and the glorious spring will come without blessed Lord's return. You see this is just a little poem in itself, a complete love-lyric in anticipation of the Bridegroom's return. How soon all this may be fulfilled for us, how soon He may come for whom our hearts are yearning, we do not know. We have waited for Him through the years; we have known the cold winters, the hard and difficult days; we have known the trying times, but oh, the joy, the gladness when He comes back! He has said, **"A little while and He that shall come and will not tarry."**

"A little while' – the Lord shall come,
and we shall wander here no more;
He'll take us to His Father's home,
Where He for us is gone before -
To dwell with Him, to see His face,
And sing the glories of His grace."

We shall then share the glory that He went to prepare. What will that mean for us and for Him! He will have the joy of His heart when He has us with Him.

The closing verses speak of that which should be going on during all the time of His absence. In the first place, we ought to be enjoying Him anticipatively, and then there should be self-judgment, putting out of the life anything that would grieve or dishonor Him. The Bridegroom speaks; may He speak to our souls. "*"O My dove, thou art in the clefts of the rock."* That is where we are resting, in the cleft of the rock.

"Rock of Ages, cleft for me,

Grace hath hid me safe in thee."

Verse 14 - "O My dove, *who art* in the clefts of the rock, in the secret places of the stairs, let me see thy countenance, let me hear thy voice; for sweet *is* thy voice, and thy countenance *is* comely, or, "in the hidden places of the going up."
15 – Take us the foxes, the little foxes, that spoil the vines; for our vines *have* tender grapes.

We are moving forward from day to day, soon to be with Himself. Have you heard Him saying these words to you, and have you sometimes turned coldly away?

Probably when you arose one morning you heard Him say, **"Let Me see thy countenance before you begin the work of the day; spend a little time with Me, let Me hear thy voice; talk with me before you go out to speak to other people; let Me enjoy a little time with you, the one for whom I died, before you take up the affairs of the day."** And have we just turned coldly away, looked at your watch, and said, "I am sorry, but I cannot spare any time this morning; I must hasten to the office or the shop," and so all day He waited for you. When evening came, He spoke again and said, "Let Me see thy countenance, let Me hear thy voice," and you said, "Oh, I am so tired and weary tonight, I have to hurry off to bed." Have there not been many days like that? Are there going to be many more? Or will you seek by grace to respond to the love of His heart and let Him see your face and hear your voice a little oftener?

Then we have her response, **"Take us the foxes, the little foxes, that spoil the vines: for our vines *have* tender grapes."** You see, her brothers had driven her out to be the vine-dresser. Now she thinks of that, and sees a figure there, and says, "I know how I had to watch the vines so carefully, and now I have to watch the growth of my own spiritual life. As I set traps for the little foxes, so now I have to judge in myself anything that would hinder fellowship with Him, that would hinder my spiritual growth." What are the little foxes that spoil the vine? I can tell you a good many. There are the little foxes **of vanity, of pride, of envy, of evil speaking, of impurity** (I think this though is a wolf instead of a little fox). Then there are the little foxes **of carelessness, of neglect of the Bible, of neglect of prayer, of neglect of fellowship with the people of God.** These are the things that spoil the vine, that hinder spiritual growth. Deal with them in the light of the tree (cross) of Yeshua; put them to death before they ruin your Christian experience, do not give them any place. "Take us the foxes, the little foxes, that spoil the vines."

And now we have the closing words, (The Shulamite speaks) Vs. 16 - "My beloved is mine, and I am his; he feedeth among the lilies." We need to be reminded of this again and again. The most intimate, sweet, and unsullied spiritual relationship is brought before us here. And this is to continue. **Vs. 17 – Until the day break, and the shadows flee away, turn, my beloved and be thou like a roe or a young hart upon the mountains of Bether," (that is, the mountains of separation.)** He is the object of her soul as she abides upon the mountains of separation until he comes back.

Oh, that these things were more real with us all! We profess to "hold" the truth of our Lord's near return. But does it hold us in such a way that we esteem all earthly things but loss for Him who is so soon to claim us wholly for Himself?" **"Let us search and try our ways,"** and make sure that we allow nothing in our lives that destroys the power of this **"blessed hope"** over our souls.

Chapter Three
Sought, But Found Him Not

Song of Songs – Chapter 3:1: - **"By night on my bed I sought him whom my soul loveth. I sought him, but I found him not."**

The third chapter of this exquisite book is divided into two parts; the first comprises verses 1 to 5, and the second, the balance of the chapter, verses 6 to 11. The opening section which we now consider sets before us communion interrupted and renewed.

First Section:
(The Shulamite Tells of Her Troubled Dream)
> 3:2 I will rise now, and go about the city in the streets, and in the broad ways I will seek him whom my soul loveth. I sought him, but I found him not.
> 3 The watchmen that go about the city found me, *to whom I said,* Saw ye him whom my soul loveth?
> 4 It *was* but a little *while* that I passed from them, but I found him, and would not let him go, until I had brought him into my mother's house, and into the chamber of her who conceived me.
> (Solomon speaks)
> 5 I charge you, O ye daughters of Jerusalem, by the roes, and by the hinds of the field, that ye stir not up, nor awake my love, till it please.

"The Art of Intimacy" is the study of sex in a marriage. This chapter deals with those who waited for marriage to have sex and those who did not. Why is sex such a large part of life, yet people are afraid to talk and teach about it from God's Word? God created sex and He knows the best way for it to be enjoyed. The Art of Intimacy deals with who should take the lead in the relationship, how to have a godly wedding and how to be romantic.

We are told just what it was that had disturbed the fellowship of the lovers. It may have been the absence of the Beloved, resulting in a temporary lethargic condition on the part of his espoused one. Possibly the entire section is to be treated as a dream. In fact, this seems the most likely explanation. But dreams often reflect the disturbed state of the heart. **"A dream cometh through the multitude of business." Eccles. 5:3.**

The opening verse depicts the restlessness of one who has lost the sense of the Lord's presence. What person has not known such experience? David once exclaimed, **"Lord, by thy favor Thou hast made my mountain to stand strong; Thou didst hide Thy face, and I was troubled." Psalm 30:7.** This withdrawal of the light of His countenance is not necessarily in anger. Sometimes it is admonitory. It is love's way of bringing the soul to a realization of something cherished or allowed that grieves the Holy Spirit of God. Or it may be the testing of faith to see whether one can trust in the dark as well as in the light. Rutherford's experience is depicted thus:

> "But flowers need night's cool sweetness,
> the moonlight and the dew;
> So Yeshua from one who loved Him,
> His presence oft withdrew."

To His disciples He said, when He announced His going away, **"Ye believe in God, believe also in Me."** That is to say, **"As you have believed in God whom you have never seen, so when I am absent believe in Me. I will be just as real – and just as true – although to sight unseen."** For though the soul loses the sense of His presence nevertheless He still abideth faithful. He never forsakes His people though He seems to have withdrawn and He does not manifest Himself. This is indeed a test of faith and of true-hearted devotion. We say, **"Absence makes the heart grow fonder,"** but there is often greater truth in the old Proverb, **"Out of sight, out of mind."** When the Lord as a boy stayed in the temple, even Mary and Joseph went on "supposing Him to be in the company," not realizing the true state of affairs.

Here the Bride feels her loss. She seeks for him, he is not

there. There is no response to her cry. For her, rest is impossible with this awful sense of loneliness upon her. She must seek until she finds; she cannot be contented without him. Would that this were always true of us! But, alas, how often we go on bereaved of the assurance of His presence, yet so insensate that we scarcely realize our loss. Here there is energy – determination – action! She *must* find him who is all in all to her. Love abhors a vacuum. Only the sense of his presence can fill and satisfy her heart.

In her dream – or possibly in reality – she leaves her mountain home and goes forth in search of the object of her deep affections. To the city she wends her way, and wanders about its streets and peers into every hidden place, looking only for Him! But at first her search is unrewarded. In fact it is not until she bears witness to others of his preciousness that he gladdens her vision. Not the terms used: **"I sought him; I found him; I will seek him; I found him not."**

The watchmen, guarding the city at night, are surprised to see a lovely and yet apparently respectable woman going about at such an hour. But she turns eagerly to them ere they reprove her, crying in the distress of her soul, **"Saw ye him whom my soul loveth?"** The abrupt question conveyed little information indeed. To the prosaic guardians of the peace, it must have sounded almost incoherent. But to her it was all that was necessary. There was only one for whom her soul yearned. Surely they too would know his worth! But, from them, she gets no response.

Leaving them, she has scarcely gone from their sight ere she comes upon the object of her search. In an ecstasy of rapture she lays hold of him, and clinging to him as to one who might again vanish away, she brings him into her own home where she first saw the light of day.

The more the passage is pondered, the more evident it seems to be that all this happened in a dream. But it tells of the deep exercises of her soul. She misses him; she cannot be happy without the sense of his presence. Her only joy is found in abiding in his love. She finds him when she seeks for him with all her heart.

This is what gratifies him. And so again we have the refrain of satisfied love. **"I charge you, O ye daughters of Jerusalem, by the roes and by the hinds of the field, that ye stir not up nor wake my love until she please."** Verse 5, for, as previously mentioned, the expression here is in the feminine in the original. Nothing gives our Lord more delight than to find a heart that joys in Him for what He is in Himself. Too often we think rather of His gifts, the gracious favors He bestows. It is right and proper that these should stir us to thanksgiving; but it is as we get to know Himself and to joy in His love that we really worship in blissful communion.

> "The bride eyes not her garments,
> but her dear Bridegroom's face;
> I will not gaze at glory,
> But on my King of Grace!
> Not at the crown He giveth,
> But on His pierced Hand;
> The Lamb is all the glory
> Of Immanuel's land."

The latter part of the chapter is of an entirely different character, and sets forth the truth of union rather than of restored communion. It is a little gem, complete in itself. The espoused one has waited long for the return of the shepherd whose love she has prized above all else. His promise to return for her has been cherished and relied upon, even though at times his continued absence has made the heart sick with yearning and ever overwhelmed the drooping spirit with fear. But never has she really lost confidence in his plighted word. Eagerly she has awaited the fulfillment of his promise.

One day all the simple folk of the countryside are astir and filled with interest and wonder as they behold a grand procession winding its way along the highway up from the glorious city of God. Outriders and trumpeters on prancing chargers herald the approach of a royal equipage. **"Who is this that cometh?"** It is a bridal procession. But who is the honored maiden called to share the love of the King? Evidently at first they look in vain for a sight of her. Everything proclaims a nuptial parade, but no bride is really seen.

The bridegroom, however, is clearly in evidence. It is the son of David himself. In excited admiration the wondering people exclaim: "Behold his palanquin, which is Solomon's!" The royal conveyance is recognized. Sixty valiant soldiers guard their King as he journeys through the country. Clad in armor, each with his sword ready to defend his sovereign against any lurking traitorous foes, they move on in orderly array, as the excitement among the Shepherds and vine-dressers grows even more intense. Not often have their eyes been regaled by such a scene as this! Perhaps they will never see it's like again!

How magnificent, how costly is that royal palanquin! It is the King's provision for the comfort of his bride. And that bride is half-hidden among the rest of the country-folk, not daring to believe that such honor is for her. All eyes are on the King. It is his crowning day – his nuptial hour – the day of the gladness of his heart. He has come forth to seek and claim his spouse whom he won as the shepherd, and to whom he now reveals himself as the King.

There is no actual mention of the claiming of the bride and bringing her to the King. It is true. But it is clearly implied. He has come to fulfill his promise to make her his own. With deep and chastened joy she responds to the royal summons and takes her place at his side, and so the procession sweeps on, leaving the bewildered on-lookers gasping with startled amazement at the sudden change in the estate of her who had been through the years but one of themselves. It is a worthy theme for a Song of Songs.! And most graphically it portrays the glorious reality which the Bride of the Lamb shall soon know when the Shepherd-King comes to claim His own.

> "He is coming as the Bridegroom,
> coming to unfold at last
> The great secret of His purpose,
> Mystery of ages past;
> And the Bride, to her is granted,
> In His beauty now to shine,
> As in rapture she exclaimeth,
> 'I am His, and He is mine!'
> Oh, what joy that marriage union,
> Mystery of love divine;
> Sweet to sing in all its fullness,
> 'I am His, and He is mine!'"

How short then will seem the waiting-time; how trifling the follies of earth which we gave up in order to be pleasing in His sight! How slight too will the sufferings of the present time appear, as compared with the glory then to be enjoyed.

In some fancy we have drawn too much upon imagination as we have sought to picture the real back ground of these lovely lyrics, let me ask, is it possible to mistake the picture when all Scripture tells the same story? What was the marriage of Adam and Eve intended to signify? What shall be said of the servant seeking a bride for Isaac, and what of the love of Jacob as he served so unwearied for Rachel? Of what "great mystery" does Asenath, the Gentile wife of Joseph, speak? And what shall be said of the love of Boaz for Ruth? Hosea who bought his bride in the slave-market gives a darker side of the picture, yet all is in wonderful harmony. All alike tell the story that **"Yeshua loved the Church and gave Himself for it, that He might sanctify and cleanse it by the washing of water by the word, and present it unto Himself a glorious Church, not** having spot, or wrinkle, or any such thing." Ephesians 5:26,27. "**All fair**" indeed will she then be in His eyes, and one with Him forever, for, "It is written, for this cause shall a man leave his father and his mother and shall be joined to his wife, and they twain shall be one flesh. This is a great mystery, but I speak concerning Christ and the church." Ephesians 5:31-32.

Surely all this should speak loudly to our hearts, we who through grace have been won for One we have never yet seen, but of whom we read, **"Whom having not seen, ye love; in whom, though now ye see Him not, yet believing, ye rejoice with joy unspeakable and full of glory."** What will it be when we behold Him coming in royal array to claim us as His very own, when we discern in the King of Kings, the Good shepherd who gave His life for the sheep, and who, ere He left this scene, gave the solemn promise, **"If I go... I will come again and receive you unto Myself."** That glad nuptial hour draws on apace. Well may our hearts be stirred and our spiritual pulses quickened as we join the wondering cry, "Who is this that cometh?"

When the Bride is caught away, what will the astonishment be on the part of those who had never understood that she was the loved one of the Lord Most High? When they realize that the Church is gone and the heavenly procession has passed them by, what will be their thoughts in that day?

Song of Songs – Chapter 3: 6-11
(The Bride speaks)
7. Who is this that cometh out of the wilderness like pillars of smoke, perfumed with myrrh and frankincense, with all powders of the merchant?
   (An officer of King Solomon's Guard Replies)
8. Behold his bed, which *is* Solomon's; threescore valiant men are about it, of the valiant of Israel.
9. They all hold swords, *being* expert in war; every man

PS_BX05630266

CreateSpace
7290 Investment Drive Suite B
North Charleston, SC 29418

Question About Your Order?
Log in to your account at www.createspace.com and "Contact Support."

05/31/2016 10:27:28 AM
Order ID: 129126805

Qty.	Item
	IN THIS SHIPMENT
1	An Epic Love Story 1532772351
1	Are They? 153005575X
1	C-ing Bible Hi 1530333792
1	Everyday Life in Biblical Times 15306
1	Garden of the Heart 15 466
1	Yo 5403
1	ift Up Mine Eyes 15 4249
1	In His Arms – Childrens Stories 1 61984
1	ross, The Sta 93473
1	e Jewish Wedd 1523248696

From Nathan
Received
June 7, 2016

hath his sword upon his thigh because of fear in the night.
10. King Solomon made himself a chariot of the wood of Lebanon.
11. He made its posts *of* silver, the bottom of it *of* gold, its covering of purple, the midst of being paved *with* love, from the daughters of Jerusalem.
(The Daughters of Jerusalem Sing)
12. Go forth, O ye daughters of Zion, and behold King Solomon with the crown with which his mother crowned him in the day of his espousals, and in the day of the gladness of his heart.

Proverbs 5:18 - "As a loving hind and a graceful doe, Let her breasts satisfy you at all times; Be exhilarated always with her love.

But we must pause here for the present. The next chapter give us the glad recognition and the happy response.

Chapter Four
No Spot in Thee

Song of Songs – Chapter 4:1-7
(Solomon, the Bridegroom Expresses His Message of Love)
1. Behold, thou *art* fair, my love; behold, thou *art* fair. Thou *hast* doves' eyes within thy locks; thy hair *is* as a flock of goats, that appear from Mount Gilead.
2. Thy teeth are like a flock *of sheep that are even* shorn, which came up from the washing, of which everyone beareth twins, and none is barren among them.
3. Thy lips are like a thread of scarlet, and thy speech *is* comely; thy temples are like a piece of a pomegranate within thy locks.
4. Thy neck *is* like the tower of David builded for an armory, on which there hang a thousand bucklers, all

shields of mighty men.
5. Thy two breasts *are* like two young roes that are twins, which feed among the lilies.
6. Until the day break, and the shadows flee away, I will go up to the mountain of myrrh, and to the hills of Franklincense.
7. **"Thou art all fair; my love; there is no spot in thee"**

It is not strange that as we think of our Lord Jesus Christ, the Heavenly Bridegroom, our souls are moved to their deepest depths, but it is hard for us to realize that He has a greater love for us than we could ever possibly have for Him. And so here in this fourth chapter of the Song of Songs, we hear the Bridegroom expressing to his loved one the feelings of his heart toward her, and as we read these words, as we listen to these heart-breathings, we should remember that the speaker is really our Lord Jesus Christ, and that the bride may be looked at in various ways, as we have already seen. Prophetically, we may think of the Bride as representing any saved soul, and the Lord expressing His delight in the one He has redeemed to Himself by His precious blood; or as that Church which Christ loved and for which He gave Himself.

So we may see in these utterances His delight in His Church. In verses one to seven of this fourth chapter, you will notice that He addresses Himself directly to the Bride, and He speaks of her beauties as He sees them in a very wonderful way. The imagery, of course, as throughout this book, is strictly oriental, and goes considerably beyond what we prosaic occidentals are in the habit of using. And yet as we read it, we see that there is nothing coarse, nothing that would bring the blush to the cheek of modesty. It is the fullest, most rapturous delight of the Bridegroom in the Bride, but every expression is in keeping with the holiness of this blessed little book.

First, he speaks of her general appearance. Four times

over in this chapter, he tell her of her fairness. Twice he declares it in verse one. He says, **"Behold, thou art fair, my love; behold, thou art fair."** In verse seven we read, **"thou art all fair, my love; there is no spot in thee."**

Song of Songs – Chapter 4:8-16
(The Bridegroom Speaks)
8. Come with me from Lebanon, my spouse, with me from Lebanon; look from the top of Amana, from the top of Senir, and Hermon, from the lions' dens, from the mountains of the leopards.
9. Thou hast ravished my heart, *my* sister, my spouse; thou hast ravished my heart with one of thine eyes, with one chain of thy neck.
10. How fair is thy love, my sister, my spouse! How much better is thy love than wine! And the fragrance of thine ointments than all spices!
11. Thy lips, O *my* spouse, drop like the honeycomb; honey and milk are under thy tongue, and the scent of thy garments is like the fragrance of Lebanon.
12. A garden enclosed *is* my sister, *my* spouse; a spring shut up a fountain sealed.
13. Thy plants are an orchard of pomegranates, with pleasant fruits; henna, with spikenard.
14. Spikenard and saffron; calamus and cinnamon, with all trees of frankincense, myrrh and aloes, with all the chief spices;
15. A fountain of gardens, a well of living waters, and streams from Lebanon.
16. **Awake, O north wind, and come thou south; blow upon my garden,** *that* **its spices may flow out.**

Again in verse 10, **"How fair is thy love, my sister, my spouse! How much better is thy love than wine!"** And yet she had no fairness in herself, as we had no beauty in ourselves. In an earlier chapter we heard her say, **"I am**

black as the tents of Kedar, as the curtains of Solomon." But he says, as he looks at her through love's eyes, **"Thou art all fair."** Does it not bring before us the wondrous thing that our Savior has done for every one of us who have been redeemed by the precious blood of Christ? We would never have been saved at all if we had not realized in some measure our own wretchedness, our own sinfulness, our unlovely character. It was because of this that we fled to Him for refuge and confessed that we were anything but fair, anything but beautiful. We took our places side by side with Job and cried, **"have heard of thee by the hearing of the ear: but now mine eye seeth Thee. Wherefore I abhor myself, and repent in dust and ashes." Job 42:5,6.** We knelt beside Isaiah and exclaimed, **"I am a man of unclean lips, and I dwell in the midst of a people of unclean lips." Isaiah 6:5.**

We took part with Peter and cried, **"Depart from me; for I am a sinful man, O Lord." Luke 5:8.** But when we took that place of repentance, of acknowledgment of our own natural deformity and unloveliness, He looked upon us in His grace and said, **'Thou art perfect in Mine eyes by the comeliness which I have put upon thee."** "WHAT! No spot in us, when we were stained by sin, when we were polluted by iniquity? Once it could be said of us, **"From the sole of the foot even unto the head there is no soundness in it; but wounds, and bruises, and putrefying sores: they have not been closed, neither bound up, neither mollified with ointment." Isaiah 1:6.** And now His holy eyes cannot find one spot of sin, nor any sign of iniquity. Let this give us to understand what grace hath wrought.

> "Amazing grace, how sweet the sound,
> That saved a wretch like Me!"

It is only God's matchless grace that has thus made us accepted in the Beloved.

Then you will notice that the Bridegroom looking upon

his Bride speaks of her person in the most glowing terms, referring to seven different things. First, he speaks of her eyes and says to her, **"Thou hast doves' eyes within thy locks."** What does that mean? The dove was a clean bird, the bird of love and sorrow, the bird offered in sacrifice upon the altar, and thus typified our Lord Jesus (Yeshua) as the heavenly One. And now he sees reflected in his Bride that which speaks of himself. **"Thou hast doves' eyes."** We may not have stopped to realize it, but the dove is very keen of sight.

Recently in an Eastern city, a poor carrier pigeon fell exhausted on one of those high buildings, and somebody working on the roof of the building caught it utterly unable to rise. They found attached to it a message that had come over three thousand miles, and that little dove had seen its way all along the miles, and had flown on and on until at last it has brought the message to that Eastern city. When our blessed Lord says to us, **"Thou art fair, My love; behold, thou art fair; thou hast doves' eyes within thy locks,"** it means not only that we have eyes of beauty, but eyes quick to discern the precious and wonderful things that are hidden for us in His Holy Word. Do we respond to this, or do those doves' eyes sometimes take to wandering, going out after the things of a poor Godless world?

He says, **"Thy hair is as a flock of goats, that appear from Mount Gilead."** He refers to the Syrian goat with its long silken hair. One can imagine the beauty of the scene, a flock of goats up yonder on the mountain-side. The Bridegroom says, **"Your hair reminds me of that."** Hair, in Scripture is a woman's glory. That is one reason why she is not supposed to follow the styles of the world and cut away her beauty and glory. You remember the woman of old who loved Yeshua and knelt at His feet and washed them with her tears and wiped them with her hair. She was using that which spoke of her beauty and her glory to minister to Him, the loving, blessed Savior. Some of my sisters will forgive me if

I say that it would be difficult for them to dry anyone's feet with their hair! Yes, her hair is a *woman's glory and beauty, and, incidentally,* that is exactly the reason why the Word of God tells the woman to cover her head when she comes into the presence of the Lord. When she comes in before Him whose glory fills the heavens, to join with His worshiping people, she is to cover her own glory that no one's attention may be distracted, but fixed on Yeshua Himself. When you get the inwardness of these things, you find there is a beauty and a privilege in them that does away with all legality, and also does away with leaving us free to follow our own judgment. In Scripture, some things are commanded because they are right, and other things are right because they are commanded. When He makes known His will, the subject Christian bows to His word, assured that there is a reason for it, though he does not always understand it. How He delights to behold His obedient people; how He glories in their moral beauty!

Then in the third place, he speaks of her teeth, and we may think that strange, but there is nothing more beautiful than a lovely set of pearls half-hidden in the mouth. **"The teeth are like a flock of sheep that are shorn, which came up from the washing; whereof every one bear twins, and none is barren among them."** The two sets of teeth answer to the twins in their cleanliness and sparkling beauty, so attractive in his eyes. And how important the teeth are, spiritually speaking, because they speak to us of mastication, of the ability to properly lay hold of and digest our food. I am afraid there are a number of toothless Christians from the standpoint. Some say, **"I do not know how it is, but other people read their Bibles and find such wonderful things, when I do not find much in mine."** The trouble is you have such poor teeth, you do not masticate your spiritual food properly. It is by meditation that we appropriate our daily provision. David said, **"My meditation of Him shall be sweet." Psalms 104:34.** Until he gives you a new set of spiritual teeth, you had better use some secondhand ones. Thank God for what others have found; read their books, and get some second-hand ones. Thank God for what others have found; read their books and get something that way! By-and-by if you will wait on Him, the Lord will give you back your teeth, even if you have lost them, and you will be able to enjoy the truth for yourself.

The third verse is most lovely: **"Thy lips are like a thread of scarlet, and thy speech is comely."** This is different from that abominable custom of today that leads so many women, of course not consistent Christian women, but those of the world and Christians living on the edge of the world, to put that filthy stuff upon their lips that makes them look like a cross between poor, low women of the street and circus performers. Here it is the red lip of health. **"Thy lips are like a thread of scarlet, and thy speech is comely."** *Why?* Because it is speech that has to do with Him! The Bride loves to speak of the Bridegroom, as the Christian loves to speak of Yeshua, and her lips are like a thread of scarlet, for she exalts that blood by which she has been brought nigh to God. Every real *Christian will have lips like a thread of scarlet, for he gladly confesses that he owes everything for eternity to that precious atoning blood of the Lord Jesus Christ.* It is not only when we gather at the table of the Lord, when we bow in worship as we take the bread and cup as from His blessed pierced hand, that we love to sing and speak and think of the blood, but always, everywhere, at all times, the believer delights to remember that he has been redeemed to God by the precious blood of Christ. You will find the scarlet thread running right through this Book.

God has said, **"The life of the flesh is in the blood, and I have given it to you upon the altar to make an atonement for your soul; it is the blood that maketh an atonement for the soul." "When I see the blood, I will pass over you." "We have been redeemed to God by the** precious blood of Christ (Yeshua), as of an unblemished spotless lamb, foreknown indeed from the foundation of the world, but manifest in these last times for you." "The blood of Jesus Christ (Yeshua), God's Son, cleanseth us from all sin." And when at last we get home to heaven, our lips will be like a thread of scarlet still, for we will join in that new song and sing our praises to Him who was **"slain and has loosed us from our sins in His own blood,"** and we will render adoration unto the Lamb whose blood was shed, that we might be made Kings and Priests unto God. O Christian, make much of the blood, speak often of the blood. Do not be satisfied with the namby-pamby, bloodless religion of the day. When you ask the question, **"Are you a Christian?"** and you get the ready answer, **"Oh, yes, I belong to the church,"** then see that your lips are like a thread of scarlet and ask, **"Are you trusting in the precious blood of the Lord Jesus (Yeshua) alone for salvation?"** So often you will find that the idle profession made a moment ago was only an empty thing. They are Christians in name only. There are thousands about us who know nothing of the cleansing value of the blood of Jesus.

"Thy temples are like a piece of a pomegranate within thy locks." You know the temple speaks of the dome of thought, and so the Bride's thought is about her bridegroom. She loves to think of him, to meditate upon the treasures found in his word. Then he delights in her as she delights in him.

In the next verse we have the strength of her character, given her by divine grace. **"Thy neck is like the tower of David builded for an armory, whereon there hang a thousand bucklers, all shields of mighty men."** David's tower, you see, is the place of defense, the place of strength, and the Bride here is one of those who can stand up straight and boldly look the world in the face, assured of the love and protection of her matchless Bridegroom. And so we are called upon to be **"strong in the Lord, and in the power of**

His might." The head won't be hanging down like a bulrush when our hearts are taken up with Him. There will be a boldness that is never known when out of communion with Him.

Then, last of all, in the seventh place He speaks of that which tells of affection. **"Thy two breasts are like two young roes that are twins, which feed among the lilies."** Her heart is his, her whole being belongs to him, and he rejoices in her. We may well sing:

"Jesus, Thou art enough
The mind and heart to fill;
Thy patient life – to calm the soul;
Thy love – its fear dispel.

"O fix our earnest gaze
So wholly, Lord on thee;
That, with Thy beauty occupied,
We elsewhere none may see."

As we joy in Him, we will find that He will joy in us. You remember what Faber wrote:

"That Thou should'st so delight in me
And be the God thou art,
Is darkness to my intellect,
But sunlight to my heart."

I cannot understand why He should say, **"Thou art all fair, My love; there is no spot in thee."** I cannot comprehend such matchless grace, but my heart can rejoice in it, and so I love Him in return because He first loved me.

Following this section in which we have the Bridegroom's joy in the Bride, in verses eight to eleven we have his summons to companionship with himself. The Bridegroom would call his Bride away from everything else that has occupied her in order to find in him her all in all.

"Come with me from Lebanon, my spouse, with me from Lebanon: look from the top of Amana, from the top of Shenir and Hermon, from the lions' den, from the mountains of the leopards. Thou hast ravished my heart, my sister, my spouse; thou hast ravished my heart with one of thine eyes, with one chain of thy neck. How fair is thy love, my sister, my spouse! How much better is thy love than wine! And the smell of thine ointments than all spices!" He sees her upon the mountain-side. And, you know, the mountain is the place of privilege, the place of beauty, of worldly grandeur and glory, but it is also the place of danger.

The leopard's lair is there and the lion's den, and as he beholds her there alone, he cries, **"Come with me from Lebanon...from the lions' dens, from the mountains of the leopards."** Our blessed Lord wants the companionship of His redeemed people. How sweet those words, **"Come with Me!,"** and you cannot afford, you who love His name, to draw back, to say, **"There are other things so lovely, so beautiful, that my soul must have; I cannot leave them to go with Thee."** He who died for you, He who left heaven's glory in order to redeem your soul, calls to you and says, **"Come with Me."** Can you draw back and say, **"No; it is too much to ask; I cannot leave these surroundings; I cannot leave these worldly follies; I cannot quit this place of danger for Thy sake, Lord Jesus?"** Surely there is not very much love there. You need to get down before Him and confess the sin of your cold-heartedness and indifference, and ask for a fresh vision of the love that He manifested in the tree (cross) that your heart may be weaned away from everything else. Dr. Watts has put it:

> "He calls me from the lion's den,
> From this wild world of beasts and men,
> To Zion where His glories are,
> No Lebanon is half so fair.

Nor dens of prey, nor flowery plains,
Nor earthly joys, nor earthly pains,
Shall hold my feet or force my stay,
When Christ invites my soul away."

Does your heart respond to that? What He desires above everything else is to see His people finding satisfaction in His company.

And then in the closing two verses of this section, verses ten and eleven, we read, **"How fair is thy love, my sister, my spouse! How much better is thy love than wine! And the smell of thine ointments than all spices! Thy lips, O my spouse, drop as the honeycomb; honey and milk are under thy tongue' and the smell of thy garments is like the smell of Lebanon."** You remember in the first chapter it is she who said, looking up to him, **"We will remember thy love more than wine."** Now it is he who responds to her and says, **"How much better is thy love than wine! And the smell of thine ointments than all spices! Thy lips, O my spouse, drop as the honeycomb; honey and milk are under thy tongue; and the smell of thy garments is like the smell of Lebanon."** His people should be fragrant with the sweetness of Christ. It is said of the disciples of old, **"they took knowledge that they had been with Jesus," (Yeshua),** and if we are in His company, there will be a rich fragrance of holiness, of heavenliness, about us wherever we are found.

A minister tells of riding with another preacher on top of a bus in London, England. As they came down a poor-looking street with a big factory on one side, they were halted, and they noticed the doors of the factory had opened and hundreds of girls were pouring out and making their way across the street to a lunch room; suddenly the air was filled with a sweet delightful fragrance. The visitor said, "Isn't that remarkable in a factory district here in London?, such wondrous fragrance! It seems like the odor of a great garden.

You would not think of finding such fragrance in this district." "Oh, you don't understand," said his friend; "this is one of the largest perfume-factories in all the British Isles, and these young people are working constantly among the perfumes, and everywhere they go the fragrance remains upon their garments."

Beloved, if you and I are living in fellowship with Yeshua, if we keep in touch with Him, everywhere we go His fragrance will be manifested in our lives.

As stated above – Song of Songs 4:12-15:
"A garden enclosed is my sister, my spouse; a spring shut up, a fountain sealed. Thy plants are an orchard of pomegranates, with pleasant fruits; camphire, with spikenard, spikenard and saffron; calamus and cinnamon, with all trees of frankincense, myrrh, and aloes, with all the chief spices: a fountain of gardens, a well of living waters, and streams from Lebanon. Awake, O north wind; and come, thou south; blow upon my garden, that the spices thereof may flow out. Let my beloved come into his garden, and eat his pleasant fruits.

Chapter Five
Permitted Communion

Song of Songs 5:1
(The Bridegroom Replies)
    1 – "I AM come into my garden, my sister, my spouse. I have gathered my myrrh with my spice; I have eaten my honeycomb with my honey; I have drunk my wine with my milk. Eat, O friends." We are purchased with a great price – 1 Corinthians 6:19 states: "Vs. 19 What? Know ye not that your body is the temple of the Holy Spirit *who is* in you, whom ye have of God, and you are not your own? Vs. 20 For ye are bought with a price; therefore, glorify God in your body and in your spirit, which are God's."

We have been noticing in chapter after chapter how the blessed Lord puts before us our privileges as those who are permitted to enter into communion with Himself, and how in this little section we have the believer (if you think of it as the individual), or Israel, or the Church, whichever you will, pictured as a watered garden set apart for our Lord Himself to bring forth fruit that will be to His delight. It is a lovely figure, one used on a number of other occasions in Scripture. In the fifty-eight chapter of the prophet Isaiah, God pictures His people as such a garden. In verse eleven, He says, "The Lord shall guide thee continually, and satisfy thy soul in drought, and make fat thy bones; and thou shalt be like a watered garden, and like a spring of water, whose waters fail not." This is a beautiful picture. Primarily it refers to Israel, and morally it speaks of any believer, of that which God would see in all *His saints as they walk with Him.* In the book of the prophet Jeremiah, chapter thirty-one, verse twelve, we read, **"Therefore they shall come and sing in the height of Zion, and shall flow together in the goodness of the Lord, for wheat, and for wine, and for oil, and for the young of the flock and of the herd: and their soul shall be as a watered garden: and they shall not sorrow any more at all."** It is the risen Christ (Yeshua) Himself from whom we draw abundant supplies of mercy and grace; (My two sheep dogs) but did you ever think of your own heart as a garden in which He is to find His joy? Your very life is as a garden which is to be for His pleasure. That is the figure you have here. It is the Bridegroom looking upon his Bride with his heart filled with delight as he says to her, **"You are to be for me, you are like a lovely garden yielding its fruit and flowers for me, set apart for myself."**

 "A garden enclosed is my sister, my spouse; a spring shut up, a fountain sealed." We in America are like open gardens that anybody can enjoy, but in Syria and in other parts of the old land, they have many enclosed gardens, gardens that are walled in. This is necessary in some of those countries, as otherwise they would be destroyed by marauding creatures and robbers. It is as though the Lord says, **"That is what I want My people to be, separated to Myself; I want them to have about them the wall of holiness, for I have marked them off as My own."** In the Psalms we read, **"the Lord hath set apart him that is Godly for Himself."** Some Christians shrink from the idea of separation. If it is only a legal thing, it may become mere Pharisaic with no heart to it, but if it is to Himself, if it is the soul going out to Him, if one turns away from the world for love of Him, then separation is a very precious thing indeed, and one does not need to think of it as legal bondage, for it is being set apart for God Himself. Could one think of a higher privilege on earth than that He might find His joy in us and we might find our joy in Him?

"A garden enclosed is my sister, my spouse." How satan likes to break down the wall, to destroy the principle of holy separation which would keep our hearts for the Lord alone; but what a loss it is to our own souls, and what a loss it means to Him, when His people become like a garden trodden under foot, as it were, by every wayfarer. That is what the Christian becomes who does not keep the path of separation.

Then notice the next figure. **"A spring shut up, a fountain sealed."** Pure water is a very precious thing in the far East and so often, when a spring is discovered, it is walled about, covered, and locked, and the owner of it keeps the key so that he can go and drink when he will, and the water is kept from pollution and waste. That is what our Lord would have in His people. He has given His Holy Spirit to dwell in us, and the Holy Spirit is Himself the Fountain of Water within every believer's heart, that we might be to His praise and to His glory. This living water within the garden will, of course, result in abundant fruit and flowers.

"Thy plants are an orchard of pomegranates, with pleasant fruits; camphire, with spikenard." The orchard suggests more than a mere garden of beautiful flowers; not only something fair to look at, or something that is fragrant to the senses, but something fruitful as well. What precious fruit is borne by the believer; what precious fruit is found in the heart of the one who is shut up to God! In Philippians One, the apostle tells those dear saints that he is sure that God who has begun the good work in them, will perform it until the day of Jesus Christ (Yeshua). In verses nine to eleven of this chapter of Philippians 1 **"And this I pray, that your love may abound yet more and more in knowledge and in all judgment; that ye may approve things that are excellent; that ye may be sincere and without offense till the day of Christ (Yeshua); being filled with the fruits of righteousness, which are by Jesus Christ (Yeshua), unto the glory and praise of God."** It seems to me that everyone ought to understand that a life that is lived for God is one bringing forth the fruits of righteousness. Love, purity, goodness, sweetness, kindness, compassion, consideration for others, all of these things are the beautiful fruits that grow in this garden when the living water is properly fructifying the soil. In Galatians 5:22 we have a long list of the fruit of the spirit. Challenge your own heart by asking, *"Am I producing this kind of fruit for Him, "Love, joy, peace, long suffering?"* It is that patience, you know, that makes you willing to endure. Then there is "gentleness, goodness, faith, meekness, temperance." This is the delightful fruit that our Lord is looking for in the lives of His people. He would have every one of us as a garden that produces fruit like this.

That word translated "orchard" is really similar to the Persian word for "Paradise," and it may suggest that as God has a paradise above for His own people, where they shall share His joy for all eternity, so a believer's heart when it is producing fruit like this, is for God a paradise where He finds His joy and His delight. I wonder if we think enough of that side of it. Are we not likely to become self-centered and merely think of God as serving us, the blessed Lord Jesus

(Yeshua) giving Himself for us, dying for us, rising again for us, nurturing our souls, guiding us through the wilderness of this world and bringing us at last to glory? Some of the hymns we sing are almost entirely occupied with the blessings that come to us, but these do not rise to the height of the Christian's communion at all. It is when we are through thinking about what God is doing for us, and are seeking by grace to adore the ONE who does all this for us, and are letting our lives go out to Him as a thank-offering in praise and adoration, that we truly rise to the height of our Christian privileges., then it is that He gathers these sweet and lovely fruits in His garden. It is not only fruit upon which He feeds, but it is that which gives satisfaction in every sense. **"Camphire, with spikenard, spikenard and saffron; calamus and cinnamon, with all trees of frankincense; myrrh and aloes, with all the chief spices."** Some of these plants give forth their fragrance as the rain and dew fall upon them; some of them send forth a subtle aroma where the rays of the sun are warming them. Others never exude, never give out their fragrance, until they are pierced and the sap flows forth. So is it with our lives. We need all kinds of varied experiences in order that we may manifest the graces of Christ in our behavior, and it is not only that we are to be for His delight in the sense in which I have been speaking, but we are to be for His service too, in making known His grace to a lost world.

In the next verse we read, **"A fountain of gardens, a well of living waters, and streams from Lebanon."** Let us see if we can correlate that. There is Lebanon, that backbone mountain range of Palestine, with Mt. Hermon to the North covered with snow. The streams coming down from Lebanon sink into the ground, and as they do so, springs rise here and there in vales and dells to the surface of the earth, and so the living water flows forth to refresh the thirsty soil. The living water represents, as we know from John's Gospel, the blessed Holy Spirit. Our Lord Jesus said, **"If any man thirst,** let him come unto Me and drink. He that believeth on Me, as the Scripture hath said, from within him shall flow rivers of living water. But this spake He of the spirit which they that believe on Him should receive: for the Holy Ghost was not yet given; because that Jesus (Yeshua) was not yet glorified." John 7:37-39.

Now the Spirit of God descending from above enters into our inmost being and then we have the living water springing up unto everlasting life. Our own hearts are refreshed and gladdened, and the living water in abundance flows out from us for the blessing of a lost world around. Is this not a beautiful picture? My brother, my sister, what do you know of this life in the fullness of the Holy Spirit? Far too many of us seem to be content to know that our sins have been forgiven, that we have a hope of heaven based upon some testimony that we have received from Holy Scripture. But it is more than this. We are not merely to have the assurance of our own salvation, but every one of us should be as watered gardens for Him, with streams flowing out for the refreshment of dying men and women all about us.

In what measure is your life touching others? In what measure are you being used of God to win other souls for Christ (Yeshua)? If we have to confess, as many of us would, that we have never had the privilege of winning one soul that so far as we know we have never yet given a testimony to any one that has really been blessed in his or her coming to Christ (Yeshua), let me suggest that there must be something that is hindering the outflow of the living water., Can it be that great boulders of worldliness, selfishness, pride, carnality sinful folly or covetousness are literally choking the fountain of living water, so that there is just a little trickling where there should be a wonderful outflowing? If this is the case, seek by grace to recognize these hindrances and deal with them one by one. Away with worldliness, away with pride. Who am I to be proud? What have I to be proud of? **"What hast thou that thou hast not received?"** Away with carnality, away with self-seeking, away with covetousness, away with living for my own interests, and let me henceforth live alone for Him who shed His precious blood for me and redeemed me to Himself. As I thus deal with these things that hinder the outflow of the living water, I will myself enter into a new, living, blessed and wonderful experience, and my testimony then will count in blessing to those about me, and my life will be at its best for Him.

There has been some question as to the identity of the first speaker in verse sixteen. It is very evident that the one who speaks in the last sentence is the bride, but is it the Bride or the Bridegroom in the first part of the verse? **Chapter 4:16 "Awake, O north wind; and come, thou south; blow upon my garden, that the spices thereof may flow out."** If it is the Bridegroom who is speaking, then he it is who is calling on the winds to blow upon what he calls, **"my garden,"** the heart of his bride, in order that she may be at her best for him. If, on the other hand, as I am personally inclined to believe, it is the bride who is speaking, then it indicates her yearning desire to be all that he would have her to be. Dear child of God, is that your desire? Do you yearn to be all that Christ (Yeshua) would have you to be, or are you still actuated by worldly and selfish motives that hinder communion with Him? Listen to these words again as we think of them as coming from the lips of the bride, **"Awake, O north wind."** That is the cold, bitter, biting, wintry blast. Naturally she would shrink from that as we all would, and yet the cold of winter is as necessary as the warmth of summer if there is going to be perfection in fruit-bearing. It is as though she says, **"Blessed God, if need be, let Thy Spirit breathe upon me through trial and sorrow, and difficulty and perplexity; take from me all in which I have trusted from the human standpoint; bereave me of everything if thou wilt; leave me cold, naked, and alone except for thy love, but work out Thy will in me."** The best apples are grown in Northern climates where frost and cold have to be faced.

Those grown in semi-tropical countries are apt to be tasteless and insipid. It takes the cold to bring out the flavor. And it is so with our lives. We need the north winds of adversity and trial as well as the zephyrs of the South so agreeable to our natures. The very things we shrink from are the experiences that will work in us to produce the peaceable fruits of righteousness. If everything were easy and soft and beautiful in our lives, they would be insipid; there would be so little in them for God that could delight His heart; and so there must be the North wind as well as the South. But, on the other hand we need the south wind also, and our precious Lord tempers the winds to every one of us. **"Awake, O North wind; and come, thou South; blow upon my garden, that the spices thereof may flow out."** It is a blessed thing to be in that state of soul where we can just trust ourselves to Him.

Charles Spurgeon tells of a man who had the words, "God is love," painted on his weather-vane. Someone said, **"That is a queer text to put there. Do you mean to say that God's love is as changeable as the wind?:** "Oh, no," said the other, **"I mean that whichever way the wind blows, God is love."** Do not forget that. It may be the North wind of bereavement when your dearest and best are snatched from you, but **"God is love."** It may be that the cold wind of what the world calls ill fortune will sweep away like a fearful cyclone all that you have accumulated for years, but **"God is love,"** and it is written, **"The Lord hath His way in the whirlwind and in the storm, and the clouds are the dust of His feet."** Nehemiah 1:3.

Perhaps you have been asking questions like this, **Why has God allowed the sufferings we have had to undergo? Why has He allowed these weeks and** months **with no employment and everything slipping away, the savings of years gone?"** Dear one of God, He giveth not account of any of His matters now, but,

"When you stand with Christ in glory,

Looking o'er life's finished story,"

Then He will make it clear to you, and you will know why He allowed the cold wind to blow over His garden as well as the South wind, and if you would bow to Him now and recognize His unchanging love, perhaps He would be able to trust you with more zephyrs from the South than you ordinarily experience. We are not subject enough to the will of God. We need to learn the lesson that, **"All things work together for good to them that love God, to them who are the called according to His purpose." Romans 8:28.**

"Awake, O North wind; and come, thou South; blow upon my garden, that the spices thereof may flow out." In other words, ***"Anything, Lord, that will make me a better Christians, a more devoted saint; anything that will make me a more faithful child of think so that thou canst find thy delight in me."*** Is that your thought? And then she looks up into the face of her Bridegroom and says, **"Let my beloved come into his garden, and eat his pleasant fruits."** How he delights to get such an invitation as that from His people. He responds to her immediately, for the first verse of chapter five really belongs to this section. She no sooner says, **"Come,"** he replies, **I am come into my garden, my sister; my spouse: I have gathered my myrrh with my spice; I have eaten my honeycomb with my honey; I have drunk my wine with my milk: eat, O friends; drink, yea, drink abundantly, O beloved."**

It closes with a scene of rapturous communion. And when you look up to the Beloved of your heart and say, **"Come into Thy garden and eat Thy pleasant fruits,"** He will immediately respond, **"I am come."** You will never have to wait; you will never have to give Him a second invitation. If you have any time for Him, He always has time for you.

Song of Songs – Chapter 5: 1-8

(The Bridegroom Replies)
- (1) - I AM come into my garden, my sister, my spouse, I have gathered my myrrh with my spice; I have eaten my honeycomb with my honey; I have drunk my wine with my milk. Eat, O friends.
(The Bride Concludes)
Drink, yea, drink abundantly, O beloved.
(The Bride Tells of Another Distressing Dream)
- (2) – I sleep, but my heart waketh. It is the voice of my Beloved that knocketh, saying
(The Bride Tells What the Bridegroom said)
Open to me, my sister, my love, my dove, my undefiled; for my head is filled with dew, and my locks with drops of the night.
(The Bride Continues for Herself)
- (3) I have put off my coat; how shall I put it on? I have Washed my feet; how shall I defile them?
- (4) My beloved put his hand to the latch of the door, and my heart was moved for him.
- (5) I rose up to open to my beloved; and my hands dripped with myrrh, and my fingers with sweet-smelling myrrh, upon the handles of the lock.
- (6) I opened to my beloved, but my beloved had withdrawn himself and was gone. My soul failed when he spoke. I sought him, but I could not find him; I called him, but he gave me no answer.
- (7) The watchmen that went about the city found me; they smote me, they wounded me; the keepers of the walls took away my veil from me.
- (8) I charge you, O daughters of Jerusalem, if ye find my beloved, that ye tell him, that I am sick with love.

We have a very long section before us beginning with the second verse of Chapter five and concluding with the fifth verse of Chapter eight. In this entire portion we have traced out for us in a very wonderful way the interruption of communion and its final restoration. We have already had one similar picture in this book where the Bridegroom's absence produced a temporary sense of estrangement. We have dealt with that more fully in this section where the Bridegrooms advances are coldly spurned. If we will remember that the Bride speaks of any regenerated soul and that the Bridegroom is our blessed Lord Jesus Christ, I am sure we shall have no difficulty in getting the spiritual lesson of these chapters.

We have all experienced interrupted communion. We have all known such periods of glad joy in the Lord as those brought before us in the previous chapter. But how often have we found that following almost immediately on a period of great blessing and delightful fellowship with the Lord, there may come a time of spiritual death and broken fellowship. You recall that in Israel's history they were scarcely through rejoicing over the wonderful victory at Jericho before they were wringing their hands in despair because of the defeat at Ai. How often in our Christian lives we have similar experiences. Perhaps you go to an edifying meeting where your whole soul is stirred by the singing, by the prayers, and by the ministry of the Word, and you feel as though you would never again lose sight of your blessed Redeemer's face; and yet the spirit is willing but the flesh is weak, and within a very short time you find yourself inquiring,

> "Where is the blessedness I knew
> When first I saw the Lord?"

And everything seems dark and cloudy and you no longer discern your Savior's presence. Is there anyone who has had uninterrupted communion with the Lord throughout all the years? I am sure there is not. Even if we imagined so it would simply be because we lacked that sensitiveness which would enable us to apprehend the fact that He was in some sense grieved because of our behavior.

We have a wonderfully beautiful picture here. The Bride has retired and she is drowsing, just about asleep[, and yet a bit restless, when there comes a knock at the door. It is the knock of the beloved one who has returned from a distant journey and he cries, **"Open to me, my sister, my love, my dove, my undefiled; for my head is filled with dew, and my locks with the drops of the night."** We have the same picture in the Renewed Covenant (New Testament) in the third chapter of the book of Revelation, in which we see the Lord Jesus waiting outside the door of the Laoedicean church. He says, **"Behold, I stand at the door and knock: if any man hear My voice, and open the door, I will come into him, and will sup with him, and he with Me."** But what lethargy there is! How few respond to His gracious request! And so have the Bride exclaims, **"I have put off my coat; how shall I put it on? I have washed my feet; how shall I defile them?"** There is no fretfulness about it. Why am I disturbed at this hour? Why did you not come at some other time? I have taken off my coat; why should I put it on now? I have washed my feet; why should I defile them? This refers to the Eastern Custom of washing the feet before seeking repose or sleep, for in the land they wore sandals and the upper part of the feet had no covering. In other words, she did not want to bestir herself even so much as to open the door to him. Have you never know similar experiences?

Have you never been so much concerned with your own affairs, and seeking your own ease, with self- pleasing, that when His voice called you for an hour of communion and fellowship with Him, you really repelled His advances, instead of gladly throwing open the door and saying, **"Blessed Lord, nothing else is worthwhile but to enjoy the sunshine of thy smile, to enjoy fellowship with Thyself?"**

Or has your soul mate or partner 'done you wrong' that you have "run home to Mother or Daddy" or "actually stomped out the door, never to return" or "go off with a friend and talk about him or her" when the better way was to turn to Yeshua and ask for His precious help? And there one can find grace, mercy and forgiveness?

In this instance, we may see in the Bride's behavior evidence of just such a state of soul. But then, as she lies there drowsing neither actually asleep nor awake, she discerns something that moves her heart. She says, **"My beloved put in his hand by the hold of the door."** We will not understand the simile unless we are familiar with those Eastern doors and locks. The lock was on the inside of the door, and there was an opening where the owner could, if he had the key, reach in and use the key from the inside to open the door. He comes, but he does not open the door in that way. He has asked admission and wants her to rise and open for him. She sees that hand come through the opening and the moment she does so, her heart is stirred and she cries, **"Oh, I must let him in."** And now she rises and hurries to the door and even as she lays hold of the lock, she exclaims, **"My hands dropped with myrrh, and my fingers with sweet-smelling myrrh, upon the handles of the lock,"** this refers to another Eastern custom. When a lover came to visit the one who had won his heart and found that she was not at home, or if at home, she did not respond to his advances, he covered the lock of the door with sweet-smelling ointments and left flowers as a token of his affection. And so the Bride says, **"My hands dropped with myrrh, and my fingers with sweet-smelling myrrh."** It was not a dream, he had really been there and had gone. But she threw the door open to enable him to hear her cry, **"Come, come in!"** but there was no answering response, **"My beloved,"** she said, **"had withdrawn himself and was gone."**

<u>Love is very sensitive</u>. The trouble with many of us is that we fail to recognize this. We have an idea that the beloved one should be ready whenever we are for a time of gladness together, but it is not always so. And so, sometimes when He comes to the heart's door we practically say, **"No,**

it is inconvenient. I do not want to drop things right now." But later when we would enjoy His presence we find He has gone. Have you never had such experiences? Has He come to you and said, "I want you to sit down with Me over My Word; I want you to spend a little time in prayer; to dismiss other things from your mind and commune with me," and you have said, "Oh, but I have so much to occupy me; I cannot do it now." Plenty of time for self but very little for Him. And then some wonderful token of His loving-kindness came to you, and you said, "Oh, I must respond to His heart," and you threw open the door as it were and called, but He was not there. And did you ever know what it was to go on for days and weeks without any real sense of His presence? "My beloved had withdrawn himself." If you do not respond to His voice when He comes to you in tender grace, you may seek Him for a long time before you will enjoy fellowship with Him again. Such is the sensitiveness of love,. He wants to make you feel that His love is worthwhile, and wants to test you as to whether you are really in earnest when you profess to desire fellowship with Him.

And so as the story goes on she leaves the house and goes out into the city seeking after him, and as she makes her way from street to street, perchance calling his name and looking here and there and wondering where he has hidden himself, she says, **"The watchmen that went about the city found me, they smote me, they wounded me; the keepers of the walls took away my veil from me."** You will always have to suffer if you refuse obedience to the voice of Yeshua when He calls you. You will always have to be tested before communion is restored.

There is a word in the Renewed Covenant (Testament) that has trouble some of our sisters. In 1 Corinthians 11 we are told that a Christian woman, when she is engaged in worship with the people of God or in public prayer or testimony, is to cover her head with a veil. And people say,

"**Why the veil?**" The Bible says that the veil is her "**POWER.**" Is that not a strange thing? In the margin of our Bible we have a rather peculiar interpretation of that. I think it must have been suggested by a man. It says, "**POWER, a sign that she is under the POWER of her husband.**" But I do not think that is it, at all. This verse, I believe, explains what it means. The covering on her head is her power. In what sense"? Look at it this way. As long as her head was veiled that was her power, but when the keepers saw her going about the streets at night, they misunderstood her motive and character, and they took away her veil. the unveiled woman was marked out as one who was unclean and unchaste, but the covering on her head was the sign of the chaste and modest wife or maiden.

Years ago my Nephew was a Salvation Army officer. He remembers that an Army girl could go anywhere with those little blue bonnets. He never knew but one in all the years he was connected with them, who was insulted by anyone in any place as long as she had that little blue bonnet on. He had been seeking the lost in the lowest kind of dives on the Barbary Coast of San Francisco, and have seen them come in with their papers and go from one rough ungodly man to another, and ordinarily no one ever said an unkind or a wicked word to them., But once a drunken sailor dared to say something insulting to one of them, immediately practically the entire crowd jumped on him and knocked him down and gave him such a bouncing as he had never had before, and then threw him in to the street for the military police to pick up. The little blue bonnet was the "power" of the Salvation Army lassie. Just so the covered head of the women in that oriental land. The uncovered head bespoke of the immoral woman, while the covered head was her power, and told that she was seeking to live a life of goodness and purity. So here, because the Bride has lost the sense of her Bridegroom's presence, she is branded as though she were impure and unholy. This shame has come upon her because she did not immediately respond to her Bridegroom's call.

Song of Songs – Chapter 5:9
(The Daughters of Jerusalem Speak)
"What *is* thy beloved more than *another* beloved, O thou fairest among women? What *is* thy beloved more than *another* beloved, that thou dost so charge us?"

She turns for help to the daughters of Jerusalem as the morning dawns and she sees them coming down the street. <u>*"I charge you, O daughters of Jerusalem, if ye find my beloved, that ye tell him , that I am sick of love."*</u> In other words, tell him my heart is yearning for him; tell him I repent of my indifference, of my cold-heartedness and my unconcern, and want him above everything else. Christian, is that what your heart says? Are you a back sliding believer? Do you remember times when you enjoyed communion with your Lord, when life with Him was sweet and precious indeed? But alas, that fellowship has been broken, and you are saying with Job, **"Oh, that I knew where I might find Him!"** Does your heart say today, **"Tell Him that I am sick of love, that my whole being is yearning after Him; I want to be restored to Him, to the sweetness of communion?"** The daughters of Jerusalem say, **"What is thy beloved more than another beloved, O thou fairest among women? What is thy beloved more than another beloved, that thou dost so charge us?"**
This one that you say means so much to you, why is he more to you than you might expect another to be to us? The world says, **"Why is Yeshua (Christ) more to you than any other?"** Why does Yeshua (Jesus) mean so much more to us than the things that you and I have known in the world? **"Tell us that we may seek him with thee."** Then at once she begins to praise him and laud him. From verse ten to the end of the Chapter in wonderful oriental imagery she praises his kindness, his graciousness, his aptness to help, his strength,

and his tenderness. She cried, **"My beloveds is the CHIEFEST among TEN THOUSAND."** And when she thus praises him they turn again and say, **"Where has he gone? How is it that you have let him slip out of your sight if he is so much to you?"** Is that not a proper question? If Yeshua (Christ) is so precious to you, if He means so much to you, why is it that you so easily allow fellowship to be broken? Why do you so readily permit other things to come in and hinder communion?

Song of Songs – Chapter 5:10-16
(A full-length Portrait of the Bridegroom. The Bride speaks)
10. My beloved *is* white and ruddy, the **Chiefest** among **ten** thousand.
11. His head *is like* the most fine gold, his locks are bushy and black as a raven.
12. His eyes *are* like *the eyes* of doves by the rivers of waters, washed with milk and fitly set.
13. His cheeks *are* like a bed of spices, *like* sweet flowers; his lips *like* lilies, dropping sweet-smelling myrrh.
14. His hands are like gold rings, set with beryl; his belly is *like* bright ivory overlaid *with* sapphires.
15. His legs *are like* pillars of marble, set upon sockets of fine gold, his countenance is like Lebanon, excellent as the cedars.
16. His mouth *is* most sweet; yea, he *is* altogether lovely. This *is* my beloved, and this is my friend, O daughters of Jerusalem.

"Whither is thy beloved gone, O thou fairest among women? Whither is thy beloved turned aside? That we may seek him with thee?" And then instantly as she bears testimony to him, she recalls the last words he said to her before that eventful night. **"I am come into my garden,"** and her own heart was the garden, and she says, **"I know**

where he is. **My beloved is gone down into his garden, to the beds of spices, to feed in the gardens and to gather lilies."** *He has and always will have, a very blessed, a very precious love, a place in her heart,* **that no other will ever hold.** And instantly he speaks, he is right there. He had been waiting and watching for her to come to the place where he was everything to her soul, and at once he exclaims. **"Thou art beautiful, O my love, as Tirzah, comely as Jerusalem, terrible as an army with banners."** And then through all the rest of the chapter he praises her; he expresses his appreciation of her as she had expressed hers of him. In chapter seven, verses one to nine, he uses one beautiful figure after another to tell all his delight in her. It is a wonderful thing to know that the Lord has far more delight in HIS PEOPLE than we ourselves have ever had in HIM. Some day we shall enjoy Him to the fullest, some day He will be everything to us; but as long as we are here, we never appreciate Him as much as He appreciates us. But as she listens to his expression of love, her heart is assured; she has the sense of restoration and fellowship. In verse ten she says, **"I am my beloved's and his desire is toward me."** In other words, he has not turned against her. When we turn from Him, the natural thought of our hearts is that He has turned against us, but He has not. If He allows us to go through trial, it is like Joseph testing his brothers in order to see if there was genuine repentance of sin.

Three times in this little book we have similar expressions to this, **"I am my beloved's and his desire is toward me."** In Chapter two, verse sixteen, we read, **"My beloved is mine, and I am his."** In other words, have you given yourself to Him? Have you trusted Him as your Savior? If you have, He has given Himself to you. Just the very moment you give yourself to Him in faith, that moment He gives Himself to you and comes to dwell in your heart. This is the assurance, then, of salvation (conversion). **"My beloved is mine, and I am His."**

Chapter Six
Searching

Song of Songs – Chapter 6:1-3
(The Daughters of Jerusalem say that they, too, Would Seek Him)
1. Whither has thy beloved gone, O thou fairest among women? Whither has thy beloved turned aside, that we may seek him with thee?
(The Bride Concludes)
2. My beloved has gone down into his garden, to the beds of spices, to feed in the gardens, and to gather lilies.
3. I *am* my beloved's, and my beloved is mine; he feedeth among the lilies.

Then in Chapter six, verse three, she says, **"I am my beloved's, and my beloved is mine."** That is communion. I belong to him and he belongs to me, that we may enjoy one another together. And then in Verse ten of chapter seven, we read, **"I am my beloved's, and his desire is toward me."** Every doubt and every fear is gone. She has found her satisfaction in him and he finds his in her. What a wonderful picture! Shall it be only a picture, or is it to be a reality in our lives? Is it not a fact that so often we do the very things the Shulamite did? So often we turn a deaf ear to the Bridegroom's voice. We can be so busy even with Christian work that we do not take time for Him. I can be so occupied with teaching that I do not have time for prayer. I can be so taken up with preparing lessons that I do not have time to feed on the Word. You may ask, "Why, how can you prepare lessons without feeding on the Word?" It is one thing to study the Bible in order to prepare a lesson which I am to give to other people, but it is another thing to sit down quietly in the presence of the Lord and say, **"Blessed Savior, as I open Thy Book I want to hear Thy voice speaking to**

my heart. I want thee to talk to me, to express Thyself to me in tones of tender love." As I read in that attitude, He speaks to my soul, and as I lift my heart to Him in prayer, I talk with Him. That is communion.

Do not be content with the knowledge of salvation or conversion; do not be content to know that your soul is eternally secure; do not be content to know that you are serving Him in some little measure. Remember, there is something that means more to Him than all your service, and that is to sit at His feet and delight your soul in His love. As you read this description in the sixth chapter it will remind you of the fullness there is in Christ (Yeshua). It seems as though every figure is exhausted to show His wonder.

> "Join all the glorious names
> Of wisdom, love and power,
> That angels ever know,
> That mortals ever bore;
> All are too mean to speak His worth,
> Too mean to set the Savior forth."

Oh, to have the heart so occupied with Him that we shall lose sight of everything else, and Christ (Yeshua) alone will satisfy every longing of our souls!

Song of Songs – Chapter 6: 4-13
(The Bridegroom Praises His Bride, 6:4-7:10)
4. Thou art beautiful, O my love, as Tirzah, comely as Jerusalem; terrible as *an army* with banners.
5. Turn away thine eyes from me, for they have overcome me; they hair *is* like a flock of goats that appear from Gilead.
6. Thy teeth are like a flock of sheep which go up from the washing of which everyone beareth twins, and *there is* not one barren among them.
7. Like a piece of a pomegranate *are* thy temples within

thy locks.
8. There are threescore queens, and fourscore concubines, and virgins without number.
9. My dove, my undefiled, is *but* one. She *is* the *only* one of her mother, she *is* the choice *one* of her who bore her. The daughters saw her, and blessed her; *yea*, the queens and the concubines, and thy praised her.
(Solomon Cites Praise of His Bride by the Women of the Court)
10. Who is she *who* looketh forth as the morning, fair as the moon, clear as the sun, *and* terrible as *an army* with banners?
(The Bride Speaks)
11. I went down into the garden of nuts to see the fruits of the valley, and to see whether the vine flourished, *and* the pomegranates budded.
12. Before I was aware, my soul made me *like* the chariots of Amminadib.
(The Daughters of Jerusalem Speak)
13. Return, return, O Shulamite; return, return, that we may look upon thee.
(The bride asks)
What will ye see in the Shulamite?
(The Daughters of Jerusalem Respond)
As it were the company of two armies.

Song of Songs – Chapter 7:1-13
(The Daughters of Jerusalem Express their Agreement About the Bride's Unique Beauty)
1. How beautiful are thy feet with shoes, O prince's daughter! The joints of thy thighs *are* like jewels, the work of the hands of a skillful workman.
2. Thy navel *is like* a round goblet, which wanteth not liquor; they belly *is like* an heap of wheat set about with lilies.
3. Thy two breasts are like two young roes *that are*

twins.
4. Thy neck *is* like a tower of ivory; thine eyes, *like* the fishpools in Heshbon, by the gate of Bath-rabbim; thy nose *is* like the tower of Lebanon which looketh toward Damascus.
5. Thine head upon thee *is* like Carmel and the hair of thine head like purple; the king is held in the tresses.
(The Bridegroom Speaks)
6. How fair and how pleasant art thou, O love, for delight!
7. This thy stature is like to a palm tree, and thy breasts, to clusters of *grapes.*
8. I said, I will go up to the palm tree, I will take hold of its boughs; now also thy breasts shall be like clusters of the vine; and the fragrance of thy breath, like apples,
9. And the roof of thy mouth like the best wine.
(The Bride Interrupts, Telling Her Beloved that Her Delights Are For His enjoyment)
For my beloved, that goeth *down* sweetly, causing the lips of those who are asleep to speak.
10. I *am* my beloved's, and his desire is toward me.
(The Bride Expresses Her Longing to Visit Her Home, 7:11-8:4)
11. Come, my beloved, let us go forth into the field, let us lodge in the villages.'
12. Let us get up early to the vineyards; let us see if the vine flourish *whether* the tender grape appear, *and* the pomegranates bud forth. There will I give thee my love.
13. The mandrakes give fragrance and at our gates are all manner of pleasant *fruits,* new and olds, *which* I have laid up for thee, O my beloved.

Song of Songs – Chapter 8:1-14
(Sensitive of the Social Gap Between Herself and the

Bridegroom, She Implies that she is Aware Still that He Loves Her)
1. Oh, that thou were as my brother, that nursed at the breasts of my mother! *When* I should find thee outside, I would kiss thee, yea, I should not be despised.
2. I would lead thee, and bring thee into my mother's house, *who* would instruct me. I would cause thee to drink of spiced wine of the juice of my pomegranate.
3. His left hand *should* be under my head, and his right hand should embrace me.
(The Bride Quotes the Bridegroom)
4. I charge you, O daughters of Jerusalem, that ye stir not up, nor awake *my* love, until it please.
(The Past is Recalled When Baal-hamon is Revisited)
(The Bride's Brothers Speak)
5. Who is this who cometh up from the wilderness, leaning upon her beloved?
(Solomon Speaks)
6. I awakened thee under the apple tree. There thy mother brought thee forth; there she brought thee forth *who* bore thee.
7. Set me as a seal upon thine heart, as a seal upon thine arm; for love is strong as death, jealousy is cruel as sheol; its coals are coals of fire, which *hath* a most vehement flame.
(The Bride Speaks to Solomon)
8. Many waters cannot quench love, neither can the floods drown it. If a man would give all the substance of his house for love, he would utterly be rejected.
(The Bride Recounts What Her Brother Once Said)
9. We have a little sister, and she hath no breasts What shall we do for our sister in the day when she shall be spoken for?
10. If she be a wall, we will build upon her a palace of silver; and if she be a door, we will enclose her with

boards of cedar.
(The Bride Continues)
11. I am a wall, and my breasts like towers, then was I in his eyes as one that found favor.
12. Solomon had a vineyard at Baal-hamon; he leased the vineyard unto keepers; every one for the fruit of it was to bring a thousand pieces of silver.
13. My vineyard, which is mine, is before me; thou, O Solomon, must have a thousand, and those who keep its fruit two hundreds.
(The Brothers Speak Again)
14. Thou who dwellest in the gardens, the companions hearken to thy voice.
(The Bridegroom Interrupts in Pleasant Repartee)
15. Cause me to hear it.
(The Bride, In Affectionate Anticipation, Responds)
16. Make haste, my beloved, and be thou like a roe or a young hart upon the mountains of spices.

Chapter Seven
Heart Sealed

"Set me as a seal upon thine heart, as a seal as the grave; the coals thereof are coals of fire, which hath a most vehement flame. Many waters cannot quench love, neither can the floods drown it: if a man would give all the substance of his house for love, it would utterly be contemned." Song of Songs 8:6-7.

It is, of course, the love of the Bridegroom for His Bride that is thus spoken of. We have been tracing the manifestations of it throughout this little book, from the time when the shepherd first looked upon the shepherdess and his heart went out to her until the time when they were united in marriage. It is a beautiful picture, first of the love of Christ (Yeshua) reaching us in our deep, deep need, and then that glorious union with Him which will be consummated at the marriage supper of the Lamb.

Now you hear the Bride exclaiming. **"Set me as a seal upon thine heart, as a seal upon thine arm."** The seal speaks of something that is settled. One draws up a legal document and seals it and that settles it. And so Christ (Yeshua) and His loved ones have entered into an eternal relationship, and He has given us the seal, the Holy Spirit. **"Upon believing, ye were sealed with that Holy Spirit of promise."** This is **"the earnest of our inheritance until the redemption of the purchased possession."** That seal is the pledge of His love, and you will noticed that in the words that follow we have love spoken of in FOUR characteristics of love.

FIRST, there is the strength of love. **"Love is strong as death."**

SECOND, the jealousy of love. In our version we read. **"Jealousy is cruel as the grave,"** and of course that is often true of human love. It may be a very cruel thing indeed, but actually the word translated **"cruel"** is the ordinary Hebrew word for **"firm"** or **"unyielding."** It may be translated, **"Jealousy is unyielding as the grave."** **"The coals thereof are coals of fire, a vehement flame,"** and this expression, **"a vehement flame,"** in the Hebrew text is **"a flame of Jah."** That is the first part of the name of Elohim and it is one of the titles of God.

THIRD, we have the endurance of love. **"Many waters cannot quench love, neither can the floods drown it."**

FOURTH, the value of love. **"If a man would give all the substance of his house for love, it would utterly be condemned."**

FIRST let us meditate on the strength or of love; and we are thinking, of course, of the love of our God as revealed in the Lord Jesus Christ, for Christ is the Bridegroom of our souls. *"Love is strong as death."*

This He has already demonstrated. "Christ loved the Church and gave Himself for it." And that giving Himself meant going into death to redeem His own. *"Love is strong as death."* We might even say in His case, **"It is stronger than death."** For death could not quench His love. He went down into death and came up in triumph that He might make us His own, and it is of this we are reminded as we gather at the Lord's table. It is this which He wishes us to cherish in a special way when we come together to remember Him. He knows how apt we are to forget; He knows how easy it is to be occupied with the ordinary things of life, and even with the work of the Lord, and forget for the moment the price He paid for our redemption; and He would call us back from time to time to sit together in sweetest and most solemn fellowship, and meditate on that mighty love of His which is **"Strong as death."** Nothing could turn Him aside.

> "Love that no thought can reach,
> Love that no tongue can teach,
> Matchless it is!"

Because there was no other way to redeem our souls, **"He steadfastly set His face to go to Jerusalem."** When He went through that Samaritan village, they did not receive Him because they realized that there was no desire upon His part to remain among them at that time, but they saw **"His face as though He would go to Jerusalem,"** and they said as it were, **"Well, if He prefers to go to Jerusalem rather than remain here with us, we are not going to pay attention to His message. We are not interested in the proclamation that He brings."** How little they understood that it was for them, as truly as for the Jews in yonder Judea, that He **"set His face steadfastly to go to Jerusalem."** If He had not gone to Jerusalem and given Himself up to the death of the Tree (cross) there could be no salvation (conversion) for Samaritan, Jew, or Gentile. But oh, the strength of His love! He allowed nothing to divert Him from that purpose for which He had come from heaven. Before He left the glory, He said, **"LO, I COME (in the volume of the book it is written of Me.) TO DO THY WILL, O GOD." Hebrews 10:7.** And to do the will of God meant for Him laying down His life on the tree (cross) for our redemption. Do we think of it as much as we should? Do we give ourselves to meditation, to dwelling on the love of Christ (Yeshua), a love that passeth knowledge, and do we often say to ourselves, **"The Son of God loved me, and gave Himself for me?"** Oh, the strength of His love!

Then we think of the jealousy of love. I know that jealousy in these poor hearts of ours is often a most contemptible and despicable thing. Jealousy on our part generally means utter selfishness. We are so completely selfish, we do not like to share our friends with anyone else; and what untold sorrow has come into many a home because of the unreasonable jealousy of a husband of a wife, of parents, or of children. But while we depreciate a jealousy which has selfishness and sin at the root of it, there is another jealousy which is absolutely pure and holy, and even on our lower plane someone has well said that, **"Love is only genuine as long as it is jealous."** When the husband reaches the place where he says, **"I do not care how my wife bestows her favors on others; I do not care how much she runs around with other men; I am so large-hearted I can share her with everybody,"** that husband does not love his wife, and if you could imagine a wife talking like that about her husband, you would know that love is gone, that it is dead.

Love cannot but be jealous, but let us see that it is a jealousy that is free from mere selfishness and unwarranted suspicion. When we think of it in connection with God we remember that one of the first things we learned to recite was the Ten Commandments, and some of us were perplexed when we read, <u>**"I the Lord thy God am a jealous God,**</u>

visiting the iniquity of the fathers upon the children unto the third and fourth generation of them that hate Me." We shrank back from that because we were so used to thinking of jealousy as a despicable human passion that we could not think of God having it in His character. But it is He who has a right to be jealous. God's jealousy is as pure as is His love, and it is because He loves us so tenderly that He is jealous. In what sense is He jealous? Knowing that our souls' happiness and blessing alone will be found in walking in fellowship with Himself, He loves us so much He does not want to see us turning away from the enjoyment of His love and trying to find satisfaction in any lesser affection, which can only be for harm and eventual ruin. **"the end of these things is death."**

Paul writing to the Corinthian church says, **"I am jealous over you with a Godly jealousy, for I have espoused you to one husband, that I may present you a chaste virgin to Christ."** And then he gives the ground of his jealousy. **"But I fear, lest by any means, as the serpent beguiled Eve through his subtlety, so your minds should be corrupted from the simplicity that is in Christ (Yeshua)."** You see Paul was a true pastor. He loved the people of Christ's flock and knew that their only lasting joy was to be found in living in communion with their Savior; and His heart was torn with a holy jealousy if he saw them turning aside to the things of the world, following after the things of the flesh, or being ensnared by the devil. Every God-anointed pastor will feel that way.

Young believers sometimes imagine that some of us who try to lead the flock of God are often needlessly hard and severe, and they think us unsympathetic and lacking in compassion and tenderness when we earnestly warm them of the folly of worldliness and carnality. They say, "Oh, they don't understand. That old fogy preacher, I have no doubt, had his fling when he was young, and now he is old and these things no longer interest him, and so he wants to keep us from having a good time."

Let me "speak as a fool," and yet I trust to the glory of God. As young believers coming to Christ (Yeshua), the first lesson we learn is that there is nothing in this poor world to satisfy the heart, and by the grace of God we seek to give it all up for Jesus' (Yeshua) sake. The only regret we have today is that there have ever been times on our lives when we have drifted into carnality and fallen into a low back sliding state, and so allowed ourselves something which afterward left a bad conscience and a sense of broken fellowship, and we have never been happy until it is judged, and we once more are in communion with the Lord. If sometimes we speak strongly about going in the ways of the world, reminding that God has said, **"Come out from among them, and be ye separate, and touch not the unclean thing."** It is because we have learned by years of experience that there is no lasting joy, there is no true unspoiled happiness for those who walk in the ways of the world. If you want a life of gladness, a life of enduring bliss; if you want to be able to lie down at last and face death with a glad, free spirit, then we beg of you, follow the path that your blessed Lord Jesus took. Oh that we might not be turned aside but that we might rouse our souls to a Godly jealousy.

I wonder if you have ever noticed that the blessed Holy Spirit who dwells in every believer is Himself spoken of as jealous. There is a passage found in James 4:4,5, that I am afraid is not often really understood, because of the way it is translated in our version, but it is a very striking one: **"Ye adulterers and adulteresses, know ye not that the friendship of the world is enmity with God? Whosoever therefore will be a friend of the world is the enemy of God. Do ye think that the Scripture saith in vain, the Spirit that dwelleth in us lusteth to envy?"** Take that home, dear young Christian. Do not be seduced by the world and its folly; do not be turned aside from the path of faithfulness to Christ (Yeshua) by the mad rush for worldly pleasure and amusement; do not allow the flesh to turn you away and rob you of what should be your chief joy. **"The friendship of the world is enmity with God. Whosoever therefore will be a friend of the world is the enemy of God."** It is the next verse that perhaps we might not understand. **"Do ye think that the Scripture saith in vain, the Spirit that dwelleth in us lusteth to envy?"** One might gather that this expression, **"The Spirit that dwelleth in us lusteth to envy,"** was a quotation from Scripture, as though He were asking, **"Do you think the Scripture, that is. The Old Testament, saith in vain, "The Spirit that dwelleth in us lusteth to envy?"** But you can search the Old Testament from the beginning of Genesis to the end of Malachi, and you will not find those words or anything that sounds like them. So it is clear that is not what is meant. In fact, there are really two distinct questions in the Greek. FIRST there is the question, **"Do ye think that the Scripture speaketh in vain?"** Do you? Do you think that the Scripture speaks in vain? Having read its warnings and its admonitions against worldliness, against the unequal yoke, against the pleasures of sin, against following the path of the flesh, do you sometimes say in your heart, "I know it is all in the Bible, but after all, I am not going to take it too seriously?" Do you think that the Scripture speaketh in vain?

Why has God put these things in His Word? Is it because He does not love you, and desires to keep you from things that would do you good? That is what the devil told Eve in the beginning. He insinuated that God did not love her. He said, **"God doth know that in the day ye eat thereof, then your eyes shall be opened, and ye shall be as gods, knowing good and evil." Genesis 3:5.** And Eve said, **"I am going to eat of it; I will try anything once."** Is that what you have been saying too? If you can only do this or do that, you think you will have an experience you have never had before. The whole world is looking for new thrills today. Before you act, put the question to yourself, "Does the Scripture speak in vain?" It tells you that the end of all these things is death and you may be assured the Scripture does NOT speak in vain.

Then there is a SECOND question, **"Doth the Spirit that dwelleth in us jealously desire?"** And the answer is, **"Yes."** The Holy Ghost dwelling in the believer jealously desires to keep us away from the world and to keep our hearts true to Christ (Yeshua). Do you realize that you never tried to go into anything that dishonored the Lord, you never took a step to go into the world, but the Spirit of God within you was grieved, and sought to exercise you because He jealously desired to keep you faithful to Christ (Yeshua)? I am talking to Christians. If you are not a Christian, the Spirit does not swell in you, and you do not know what this is.

Our blessed Lord wants you all for Himself. People say sometimes, "Well, I want to give the Lord the first place in my heart," and they mean that there will be a lot of places for other things. The Lord does not merely want the first place; He wants the whole place; He wants to control your whole heart, and when He has the entire control, everything you do will be done for His glory. A striking little incident is told by a Pastor Dolman. Before the world war he was in Russia holding some meetings in the palace of one of the Russian nobility. Among those who attended the meetings was a Grand Duchess. She was a sincere evangelical Christian. Dr. Dolman was talking one day about a life devoted to Yeshua, about separation and unworldliness, and when he finished, the Grand Duchess stepped forward and said, "I do not agree with everything Pastor Dolman said."

"What did I say with which you do not agree. Your Imperial Highness?" asked Dr. Dolman.

"You said it is wrong to go to the theater. I go to the theater, but I never go without first getting down on my knees and asking Him to go with me, and He does."

Pastor Dolman said, "But, Your Imperial Highness, I did not say a word about the theater."

"I know; but you meant that."

"Your Imperial Highness," said Dr. Dolman, "are you not turning things around? Who gave you or me authority to decide where we will go or what we will do, and then to ask the Lord to be with us in it? Instead of getting down on your knees and saying, 'Lord, I am going to the theater, come with me' why don't you wait until He comes to you and says, 'Grand Duchess, I am going to the theater, and I want you to go with Me?'

She threw up her hands and was honest enough to say, "Pastor Dolman, you have spoiled the theater for me. I cannot go again."

"Where He leads me, I will follow," But do not you start and ask Him to tag along. Let Him lead. Because He knows that your real, lasting happiness and joy are bound up in devotion to Him, He is jealous lest you should be turned aside.

Now we notice the endurance of love. **"Many waters cannot quench love, neither can the floods drown it."** How precious that is! How blessedly it was proven in His case. He went down beneath the floods of divine judgment. He could say, **"Deep calleth unto deep at the noise of Thy waterspouts: all thy waves and thy billows are gone over Me." Psalm 42:7.** But it did not quench His love, and through all the years since His people have had to endure many things; they have had to pass through deep waters, to go through great trials.

But He has been with them through it all. **"In all their affliction He was afflicted, and the angel of His presence saved them." Isaiah 63:9.** In Isaiah 43:2 **we read, "When thou passest through the waters, I will be with thee; and through the rivers, they shall not overflow thee: when thou walkest through the fire, thou shalt not be burned; neither shall the flame kindle upon thee."** Don't you love to have somebody to whom you can go with all your troubles and know He will never get tired of you?

Some years ago a Pastor became acquainted with a poor

little lady in a place where he was ministering the Word. She was going through all kinds of sorrow, and she came to him and said, "I would just like to tell you about my troubles." He and his wife felt like saying, "Dear lady, we wish you would tell them to the Lord." But they sat down and listened, and now for over ten years they have been getting her troubles by mail, and they try to send her a little encouraging and sympathetic word in reply. Recently they meet her again and she said, "You must be getting awfully tired of my troubles," and if we had told the truth, we would have had to say, "Yes, we are," but we said, "What is troubling you now?" "Oh," she said, it is not anything new, but it is such a comfort to find people who will enter into them and understand!" And she was so effusive in her gratitude we were ashamed that we had not entered into things more deeply.

Ah, we have a great High Priest (Yeshua) who never wearies of our trials. We weary of hearing of them sometimes because they stir our hearts and we would like to do that which we cannot do; but He has power to see us through. No trial, no distress, can quench His love. **"Having loved His own which were in the world, He loved them unto the end." John 13:1.** Somebody has translated it this way, *"Having loved His own which were in the world, He loved them all the way through."* Through what? Through everything. He even loved Peter through his denial, through his cursing and swearing, and loved him back into fellowship with Himself. HIS LOVE IS UNFAILING. Having taken us up in grace. He loves to the end.

Let us look now at the VALUE OF LOVE. Can you purchase love? Can you pay for it? I was in a home at one time where a very rich man of seventy years of age, worth millions, had married a girl of eighteen. Her ambitious, worldly-minded mother had engineered the marriage. I could not help noticing that young wife off in a corner sobbing to herself and crying bitterly, but I tried never to interfere, for I did not want her to tell me what was in her heart. But one day the husband said, "Do you notice how downhearted my wife is?" I said, "She must have had some great sorrow."

"I am her sorrow," he said. "She was a poor girl, very beautiful and talented, and as you know, I have been very successful, and I just thought that I could give her every comfort and could surely make her love me. I know that we do not seem to be suited; she is so much younger than I. But she can have everything, all the beautiful clothes and jewels she wants, and surely any girl ought to be happy in a home like this. But, you know, it is all in vain; I cannot seem to buy her love."

Of course not. He ought to have known that he did not have that in his heart to which she could respond. They belonged to two different ages, as it were. **"Many waters cannot quench love, neither can the floods drown it: if a man would give all the substance of his house for love, it would utterly be contemned."** You cannot buy love, but oh, His love to us creates love in us. It is not the wonderful things that He has done for us, it is not the fact that He has enriched us for eternity, but it is because of what He is. <u>*"We love Him because He first loved us."*</u>

"His is an unchanging love,
Higher than the heights above;
Deeper than the depths beneath,
Free and faithful, strong as death."

What a blessed thing to know Him and love Him and be loved by Him! Oh, to be kept from wounding such a Lover, from grieving His Holy Spirit! For we read, **"THE LOVE OF GOD IS SHED ABROAD IN OUR HEARTS BY THE HOLY SPIRIT WHICH IS GIVEN UNTO US."**

**Chapter Eight
Responsibility for Family**

"What shall we do for our sister?" Song of Songs 8:8

This question was put by the Bride to the Bridegroom after she had been brought into the full enjoyment of the privileges that he delighted to lavish upon her. He had found her a shepherdess there in the hill country, and loved her and won her heart in those trying days when she felt herself so despised and neglected. Brought to the palace and united in marriage to the King, enjoying the fullness of his tender consideration and surrounded by the evidences of his affection, she could not keep from thinking of the little mountain home from which she had come.

She thought of the dear old mother who had raised her and cared for her after the father's death, for it is evident that the mother was a widow, and the family by superintending the King's vineyard earned a precarious living; and then she thought of the little sister, much younger than she, who had none of the privileges that she was enjoying. And as she thought of her, she seemed to say, **"This Bridegroom of mine, my King, the one who has loved me and brought me into these privileges, cannot but take an interest in my family, in my household, and I am going to speak to him about that sister of mine."** And so she turned to him in the tenderest, most confiding way, and said, **"I have a little sister, a little undeveloped sister, up there in the vineyard. I am concerned about her. Is there not something we could do for her? What shall we do for our sister?"** And he responds at once, **"If she be a wall, we will build upon her a palace of silver; and if she be a door, we will enclose her with boards of cedar."** You see, this is just the oriental way of saying, **"I am so glad you spoke to me about that little sister of yours; I am so glad that you have not forgotten her and her needs. It will be a real privilege for me to show my love for you by what I do for her."** And so he uses the striking figures of the wall and the door as he asserts his willingness to help. It was as though he said, **"Whatever her circumstances are, and whatever her needs are, I will be delighted to minister to them and I**

will make you my agent in doing it."

It seems to me this expresses one of the very first evidences of union with Christ (Yeshua). We are no sooner saved (converted) ourselves, no sooner rejoicing in the knowledge of Christ as our Redeemer, as the Lover of our souls, as our heavenly Bridegroom, than we begin to think of others less privileged, and our hearts cry out with longing. **"What about my little sister? What about my brother? What about those who are still in their sins and still in their deep, deep need, who do not know, do not understand this incomprehensible love of thine which means so much to me?"** And it is the Holy Spirit Himself who puts that yearning into our hearts that leads us to manifest an interest in the souls of others. In other words, every real Christian feels within him something that impels him to missionary service.

Are you converted yourself? Then have you been to the Lord about that little sister, or about that neglected brother? Perhaps it is a little sister or a brother you have never seen, and maybe, strange to say, of an altogether different color from yours! Perhaps that little sister of yours is away yonder, a child-widow in India, perhaps a down-trodden native woman in Central Africa, or a degraded Indian in the wilds of South America, but yet your little sister; for we read, **"God hath made of one blood all nations that be upon the face of the earth."** And while you may say, **"But she is so sinful, so undeserving,"** you must remember that you too were sinful and undeserving and the grace that is lavished upon you came from His heart of love. He delights to give to the undeserving, and the very need of that little sister of yours is the reason why you should be going to the Lord about her.

The Bride here is really praying about her sister. Do you often go to the blessed Lord in prayer for that little sister of yours? Perhaps it is a brother. My brother, you who rejoice in Christ Jesus, do you think very often of that poor, ignorant, under-privileged, degraded, sinful brother of yours, living perhaps in heathen darkness today, or dwelling in the slums of one of our great cities, or, it may be, enjoying all that this life has to offer and yet not knowing Christ (Yeshua)? Have you been to Him about that degraded one? Somebody has said, **"A selfish Christian is a contradiction in terms,"** and yet we do hear people talking about selfish Christians. Christianity is the manifestation in the life of the love of Christ, and that same love which was lavished upon you He would now have you lavish upon others in their need. What wonderful pictures we have along this line!

In the beginning of John's Gospel we read how the LORD reveled Himself to one and another, and everyone who got that divine revelation went after someone else. Each said, "I have a brother, a friend, a dear one in need, and I must go to that one and tell the story of Yeshua; tell him that we have found Him." The privileges, the blessings that God has given to us in Yeshua are not given to us for ourselves alone. We may say in connection with them: you must either use them or lose them. "What," you say, "are you telling us that we may lose our souls after having been truly converted?" That is not a blessing. Your soul is you. Of course you cannot lose that if it is converted (saved). I recognize the fact that having life eternal, you shall never perish, but I am talking about the blessings that the Lord lavishes upon you from day to day. They are in order that you may share them with others. To what extent do you enter into that?

I would have you think of three things. FIRST, to what extend do you use your time for the blessing of other people? When I find Christians who need so much physical recreation and have so little time to seek to win souls, I do not quite understand it. I was speaking with a young man some months ago, and I said, "Do you do anything to win others for Yeshua?" He said, "I would like to, but it does not seem to be my gift. I work hard all day, and when Saturday comes I have to go off and get some physical exercise." I think his great invigorating exercise was throwing horse-shoes at a little stick. I said, "Did it ever strike you that you could get wonderful exercise by taking a bundle of tracts and going out on a country road and visiting the homes along the way, telling people about their souls? Walking is wonderful exercise."

"But," he said, "you see, I am thinking of serious things all week, and I cannot be serious on Saturday afternoon." Time is given us to use in view of eternity. I quite recognize that we need a certain amount of physical exercise or we would go to pieces, but you will find you can get on beautifully if you give more of your time to God. I was converted forty-one years ago, and I can honestly say my best times ever since have been those in which I have spent my days trying to help other people to a knowledge of Yeshua, and it is the greatest exercise in the world. I was visiting a minister some time ago, and he asked, "What do you do for physical exercise?" I answered, "I teach." "But I mean when you want to get a rest," he said. "I teach some more and that rests me." I answered; "the more you do in the work of the Lord, the better you feel." "Sister," he said, "you will have a nervous breakdown if you are not careful." "But I am trying to be careful," I said. It is not the Lord's work that gives people nervous breakdowns, it is getting into debt, getting mixed up in questionable things, and then you get worried and upset. Just keep at solid service for the Lord Jesus Christ, and you will not have a nervous breakdown. Paul was at it for thirty years. They tried to kill him again and again, he was half-drowned several times, and was thrown to wild beasts, but the old man, when about seventy years of age, had much more vigor than a lot of worldly ministers that I have ever meet, who have to go on a prolonged vacation every once in a while "just to get away." Our time belongs to the Lord Jesus, and He gives it to us in order that we may use it to bless and help other folk. **"Look not every man on his own things, but every man also on the things of others."**

Philippians 2:4.
   Some time ago a friend of mine knew a dear man, one of the greatest men for physical exercise that he ever saw. He worked hard on the railroad. My friend would see him down on his knees, a great big covering over his eyes to shield them from the brilliant light, as he welded the steel rails. By Saturday noon, he was just worn out, and he would get a bundle of books and off he would go for 'exercise', over the hills and far away, hunting up poor needy souls, maybe in the County Hospital, possibly in the jails, and to poor families,. Sometimes he would hear of somebody lying sick and poor and miserable, and he would go to see that one. And you know he had a remarkable way of preaching the Gospel. He would often lay down a five-dollar bill at the side of the bed, if he found out that they had no money to pay the bills. On Saturday (Sabbath) he would say, "MY! I was worn out yesterday, but I have had a wonderful time this day (Saturday, Sabbath), and I am all rested up." He was living for others.

> "Live for others while on earth you live,
> Give for others what you have to give."

   And then you will find the secret of a really happy fulfilled Christian life. Your time is to be spent in the service of Christ for the blessing of others, for the blessing of the little sister, or that poor brother.
   And then there is something else. He has entrusted you with your talents. "Oh, but," you say, "I haven't any." Oh, yes; you have. You would not like it if others said you had none. But who are you using them for? For Christ, for the blessing of that brother, of that sister in need? It is the investment that you make of your talents here for the glory of the Lord Jesus Christ that is going to bring you a reward at His judgment-seat. You remember what He said, **"Unto every one that hath shall be given…but from him that**

hath not shall be taken away even that which he hath." You are to use the talents God has given you for Jesus' sake. Is it the ability to speak? Use it for winning souls to Christ., Is it that you know how to be a kindly sympathetic friend? Then surely you have a wonderful sphere for service. Is it looking up the shut-ins, the sick and needy, and giving them a tender loving word? You would bless and help so many you never think of now if you would only begin to use those talents for Him. It is not all the work of the man on the platform. I never see souls coming to Yeshua in a meeting but I wonder what started them. Years ago, when I was young and ignorant, I hear of ministers that went home and said – "I won six souls tonight," and their wives would look at them and say, "Are you sure YOU did it?" Then they would say, "NO," of course not, "but the Lord did and used me to teach and deliver the message." Perhaps it was the lesson taught at the knee of a mother or father. Perhaps it was the father's word dropped into the heart or perhaps a dear friend that refused to give up. There is seldom a soul who comes to Christ but there were a lot of folk who had to do with it. It is not just the friend or the minister that loved enough not to quite. God gives us talents to use. Paul planted, Apollos watered, "but God gave the increase."

Then there is the privilege not only to use time and talents, but also money, to help and bless that little sister, that neglected brother. What a wonderful thing consecrated money is when used properly! There never would have been a dollar bill, a piece of silver money, a gold, copper or nickel coin in the world, if it had not been for sin. That is why Jesus calls it the mammon of unrighteousness. Every coin in your pocket is a witness that sin has come into the world. If men and women had remained as they were when God created them, there would have been no money. People would not have sought to build up fortunes, and buy and sell things. We would still be living in a glorious state of this earth, and we would not have had to go out and earn our bread by the sweat of our brow. And now Jesus says, **"Make to yourselves friends of the mammon of unrighteousness; that when ye fail, they may receive you into everlasting habitations." Luke 16:9.** Since the money is here, and we cannot get along without it, do not live for it, do not let it get a hold on you. **"(The love of money is the root of all evil")**, but use it now in reference to the everlasting habitations, use it to meet, of course, you own needs and those of your family, but then use it as God enables you to bless and help others in their deep spiritual need and in their temporal need too. Then, by-and-by, when at last you reach the glorious habitation, you will see a throng running down the golden street to meet you and they will say, "Welcome," and you will ask in amazement, "Who can these be?" And one will answer, "We are so glad to welcome you here, for it was your dollar that paid for the Testament that brought me the message of Christ (Yeshua)." Another, "You met my need when in such distress I thought nobody cared for me, and then you gave me the money for a good dinner, and I could not help but think of the God of all grace who had put it in your heart to do that for me," and another, "I came to Jesus because of the kind deed you did for me." Then we will feel it was worthwhile that we spent and were spent for others. "What shall be done for out little sister?" Let us share with her the good things we have.

The King says, **"If she be a wall, we will build upon her a palace of silver."** A wall speaks of security. If she has already entered into the blessing of Christ, we will build upon her a silver palace. We will add to that which is already hers., We will try to help and lead her on and build her up in the things which be in Christ. **"If she be a door, we will enclose her with boards of cedar."** A door speaks of responsibility, or opportunity for service. **"A great door,"** says the apostle, **"and effectual is opened unto me, and there are many adversaries." 1 Corinthians 16:9. "Behold, I have set before thee an open door, and no man can shut it: for thou hast a little strength, and hast kept**

my word, and
Hast not denied My name." Revelation 3:8. But what use is a door if it has no side-posts to swing from? **"If she be a door, we will enclose her with boards of cedar."** If she wants an opportunity for service, we will help to make it possible, and we will assist her in whatever is required, that she may work the better for the Lord Jesus Christ.

Then as the chapter closes and the little book closes, the Bride, her heart content to think she has come into blessing and that her little sister too has come into blessing goes over the past, and talks about vineyard days, the love that has been shown and the bliss now hers, and then she turns to her beloved one and says, <u>*"Make haste, my beloved, and be then like to a roe or to a young hart upon the mountains of spices."*</u> *"Till the day break and the shadows flee away."* The consummation of all bliss will be when we are at home forever with Him. Till then, let us seek to spend and be spent for His glory.

You may have heard of the missionary offering that was being taken, and as the box was handed to a very wealthy man, he brushed it to one side and said, "I do not believe in missions." "Then," said the usher, "take something out; this is for the heathen." How can you be a real Christian and not be concerned about those who are less privileged than you are" God stir our hearts to think of the millions still in their great, great need. If we can do nothing else for them, we can bring their case to Him; we can be prayer-helpers; we can intercede on their behalf. The wonderful thing is that when you begin to pray, the rest follows. Men who pray devise ways and means for giving. A lady said one time, "You know my husband is unsaved (not converted) and he never lets me have any money. He says he would not for the world give me a dime to put in the missionary offering. But I started praying about missions, and as I prayed, there came such a burden on my heart to do something. I had two or three chickens that I had bought with a little money I received from doing some sewing for a neighbor. It was all mine, and I said, "I am going to devote one chicken to the Lord, and every egg that this chicken lays will belong to Him." It has been wonderful to me to see that the other chickens lay every once in a while, but my husband growls and says, 'That missionary chicken of yours lays nearly two eggs a day.' Of course that is an exaggeration, but every little while I have another dozen eggs, and I take them to the corner store and get my money, and that goes for missions." I believe that the Lord will take that money and do with it what He did with the five loaves and two fishes: multiply, and multiply, and multiply them. Maybe one way in which He will multiply it will be to start some of your giving, and then, you see, the Lord will turn to this lady and say, "You are the woman that had that chicken the minister told about. I am going to give you part of the reward, for these folk just copied from you!"

Let us seek by grace to make every day count for the blessing of others. Loving Him truly we cannot be selfish or indifferent to the needs of those for whom He died, "until the day break and the shadows flee away."

The ART of COMMITMENT will finish this incredible love story. Perhaps the most important aspect of this little book is the section of the sovereignty of God . He is the creator of all and He knows what is best for everyone. It is God who brings couples from initial attraction to the joy of sex to a lifelong commitment. In order to have a Godly relationship and marriage, Jesus Christ (Yeshua) must be your Lord and Savior. It is about being committed to Yeshua and then to one another.

May God bless you and keep you. Numbers 6:24

The 16 "Nevers of Communication with your Beloved"

1. Never speak rashly.
2. Never confront your spouse publicly.

3. Never confront your spouse in your children's presence.
4. Never use your children in the conflict.,
5. Never say "never" or "always."
6. Never resort to name-calling.
7. Never get historical.
8. Never stomp out of the room or leave.
9. Never raise your voice in anger.,
10. Never bring family members into the discussion unless they are a direct part of the problem being addressed.
11. Never win through reasoning or logic and never out-argue.
12. Never be condescending.
13. Never demean.
14. Never accuse your spouse with "you" statements.
15. Never allow an argument to begin if both of you are overly tired, if one of you is under the influence of chemicals, or if one of you is physically ill.
16. Never touch your spouse in a harmful manner.

Biography

Addresses on the Song of Solomon by H.A. Ironside, Litt. D.
Author of "Notes on Hebrews:
Lectures on Romans,
Colossians
Revelation

7 Feast Of The LORD Being Symbolic Of New Life

Below is an overview of how the festivals of our Heavenly Father is liken unto new life.

Feast	Christian Fulfillment	Baby Development
Passover (Pesach) Fertilization must take place within 24 hours.	New Life (Egg) Leviticus 23:5	Ovulation
Unleavened Bread Matzoh Bread is stripped	The Seed (Planting) 1 Corinthians 5:7-8 Leviticus 23:6-8	**Fertilization** Christ buried
First Fruits Spring planting Leviticus 23:10-11; (Matthew 27:27-53; Early crop of believers)	Resurrection Resurrection Day Resurrection of the entire church	**Raised from dead**
Pentecost Acts 2:1-50 days from Reed Sea. 50 days Embryo becomes a fetus. Pentecost Greek word means 50.	Harvest	**New Creature** Fetus Sweet Holy Spirit

The 4 feast (festivals) above have been fulfilled at Pentecost. Christ breathed the Holy Spirit upon the disciples.

The following 3 festivals are unfulfilled. We await their fulfillment.

Feast	Christian Fulfillment	Baby Development
Trumpets 1st day of 7th month the baby can hear.	**Catching Up (Rapture)** Joshua 6:5 1 Thessalonians 4:16-17	Hearing

Feast	Christian Fulfillment	Baby Development
Day of Atonement 10 days into 7th month fetal blood changes so that it can carry it's own oxygen.	Redemption	**Blood** Hemoglobin A
Tabernacles End of Feasts Leviticus 23:27 15th day of 7th month Normal baby has 2 healthy lungs	**Kingdom** House of Spirit Spirit in the Air	**Lungs** Baby will live if born at Tabernacles
Hanukkah	**Eternity**	**Eternal Life**

Not given by God. A days' supply of oil lasted 8 nights. It's beyond Tabernacles and beyond the Kingdom. We have eternity with God. This is the fulfillment.

Job 23:12;
12 "I don't withdraw from his lips' command; I treasure his words more than my daily food."

Ecclesiastes 12:13;
13 Now all has been heard; here is the conclusion of the matter: Fear God and keep his commandments, for this is the duty of all mankind. (NIV®)

SMILE... GOD LOVES YOU... KEEP LOOKING UP!

Made in the USA
Charleston, SC
01 June 2016